Spirit, Body, Soul Self Control
PART 1

WALKING IN STEP WITH THE SPIRIT

TABLE OF CONTENTS

PART 1 OF A 3 PART SERIES

SPIRIT
BODY
SOUL

SELF CONTROL

A WORKBOOK TO HELP DISCIPLES OF JESUS MATURE

SONJA CHLOUPEK

SPIRIT, BODY, SOUL SELF CONTROL - PART 1

Published by Best Seller Publishing®, St. Augustine, FL
Best Seller Publishing® is a registered trademark.
Printed in the United States of America.

ISBN: 978-1-969338-53-3

For more information, please write:
Best Seller Publishing®
1775 US-1 #1070
St. Augustine, FL 32084
or call 1 (626) 765-9750
Visit us online at: www.BestSellerPublishing.org

Dedication

To my Almighty God, thank you for giving us direct access to your heart through the precious blood of Jesus. **This work is for your glory alone**.

To my wonderful husband, Chris, thank you for your grit, sense of humor and deep convictions. Since April 1st, 1995 you have been my hero, best friend, lover and incredible partner in the Gospel. I am so privileged to do life by your side.

To our amazing children, Chase and Cassidi - our most treasured rewards from God. Thank you for your unconditional love and encouragement. I cherish every moment we get to share and the closeness we nurture. I am humbled and honored to be your Mama. Next to the Holy Spirit and Dad, you are my finest personal spiritual trainers and my dearest companions - I love you more than you know.

Also to every Disciple of Jesus who longs to hear the words, "Well done, good and faithful servant" - this 3 Part Workbook Series is for you.

INTRODUCTION: SPIRIT

Are you a true follower of Jesus and unsure how to grow up spiritually? Perhaps you've been a Christian for some time and find yourself struggling with frustration, depression, anxiety, monotony or fear - despite your best efforts to mature? Are you feeling "stuck" in your walk with God and longing for a breakthrough?

If so, you're not alone. This 3 Part Workbook Series was born out of that same longing in my heart. It's been a decade in the making and one of the "hardest jobs I've ever loved". My deepest desire is to be useful to our Master, helping others not only find salvation but thrive in maturing spiritually as I do the same.

I invite you to come along with me - realize the power in **Self Control** over **Spirit, Body and Soul**.

> *"Now may the God of peace make you holy in every way, and may your whole spirit and soul and body be kept blameless until our Lord Jesus Christ comes again." - 1 Thessalonians 5:23 (NLT)*

Thank you for approaching this 3 Part Workbook Series prayerfully, with great consistency, intentional humility and with an expectant faith to expand your spiritual bandwidth - refuse to stay stagnant. You're here because the Spirit in you yearns for more - more depth, more peace, more confidence in God and in your own self worth.

As you walk through the pages, go at your own pace - take time to soak in the scriptures, wrestle with the scientific insights, reflect on the personal stories and use the practical tools. Let the quotes and reflections stir your soul. Aim for quality over quantity - one simple truth applied, can lead to profound transformation. If you open your heart and mind and commit to the work, you'll experience clarity, agency and power to walk in God's peace like never before.

The structure of this series flows directly from the two greatest commandments Jesus gave us in Matthew 22:36–40:

> *"'Love the Lord your God with all your heart and with all your soul and with all your mind.' This is the first and greatest commandment. And the second is like it: 'Love your neighbor as yourself.'"*

In Part 1, we begin with what Jesus called the greatest commandment - loving the Lord. This section focuses on the Holy Spirit - how to nourish His presence within you so that your relationship with God will flourish.

In Parts 2 and 3, we turn to the second commandment, which calls us to love others as we love ourselves. Before we can pour out love to our neighbor, we must learn to love ourselves the way God does and to treat our bodies as sacred temples, this is the theme of Part 2.

Part 3 moves deeper into loving our souls - managing our emotions and inner narratives through the lens of God's truth by renewing our minds accordingly. When we direct our energy toward loving our Lord and then embracing His love for us, love for our neighbors will ring out at the perfect pitch and cadence.

So dear Reader let's "Grow Baby grow!"

MY JOURNEY

I was born and raised in the gorgeous country of South Africa and am so proud of and grateful for my amazing family - my beloved parents, Norman and Marlene Pedersen (married since 1962) as well as my wonderful siblings, Karen, Estelle, Mark and their beautiful families. In many ways we had the ideal childhood. I thank God for the solid foundation of love and devotion that my parents laid.

At just 18 years old, I set out on a grand adventure - driven by a deep longing for meaning I decided to explore the world and immerse myself into new cultures, languages and cuisines. Although I had been taught about Jesus and His sacrifice on the Cross, I was never challenged to repent and actually become a true follower or Disciple of Jesus. This left me without a purpose greater than myself and as a result self dominated - in my ignorance and rebellion I thought I had it made.

Scenic Cape Town - South Africa

My journey led me to beautiful places including England and Scotland where I had the privilege of working and connecting with some very special people. Next I traveled to France, Spain, Germany, Holland, Belgium, Italy, Austria and Switzerland and got to experience a taste of their rich histories, traditions and flavors.

One of the most unforgettable chapters was going to Israel where I volunteered on a "kibbutz" near the West Bank. We would actually go horseback riding into that area with no trouble at all, it was a blast. Google what Kibbutzim were in the 90's for more context. After a few months I moved to Tel Aviv because, let's just say, you do not make money on a Kibbutz. There I accepted a live-in nanny position with a hard working Israeli family. I loved the two little boys I got to care for, Jonny (6 months old) and Moddy (5 years old), short for Jonathan and Mordecai. I learned that when and if God would bless me with children that I wanted to spend as much time as I could raising them myself because I felt bad for the parents who were missing out on so much fun. We went on all kinds of field trips and Moddy actually

taught me how to speak Hebrew. The things we can learn from children!
Ironically it was also in the "Holy Land" that I lost my virginity - knowing that immorality was a sin, I justified it because I wasn't "struck by lightning" and "loved him and most likely would marry him". I had a form of godliness but no power or convictions to say "no" (2 Tim 3:1-5).

Sailing across the Mediterranean, now with my boyfriend, was amazing too - we visited the stunning islands of Crete and Rhodes, then made our way through scenic Greece and into the vibrant city of Istanbul. My experience in Turkey made me very grateful for where and how I was raised.

Seeing the breathtaking United States of America was another dream materialized.   I've actually had the privilege of visiting all 50 incredible States. Working my way around the world was an experience I will always treasure. Each encounter added perspective to my life's journey with much of it being exhilarating and a portion of it definitely qualifying as the "School of Hard Knocks".   When you are 10, 000 miles from your family you quickly realize that if you do not work, you will not eat. These are excellent lessons in adulting.

After 5 years of travel, on January 17th 1994 in Beverly Hills, California - I was suddenly awoken by what I had never experienced before. The ground was vigorously shaking and several items came crashing down. There was widespread damage throughout Los Angeles - collapsed buildings as well as freeways, fires, deaths and thousands injured. This was the devastation caused by the 6.7 magnitude of the Northridge earthquake. Despite my lifestyle of deliberate sin at the time, I fell to my knees and cried, "God, help me!" This would initiate a watershed period in my life where God answered my quest to find meaning and purpose for my life. He graciously redirected my attention from people and places onto my spiritual lack of well being. Soon after that desperate prayer, I encountered some real Disciples of Jesus. They were different from "Christians" I had been exposed to since they loved God by doing their best to obey Him.

The destruction of the earthquake

Their lifestyles were marked by a deep love and respect for God and His agenda. They did not engage in patterns of deliberate willful sin and when they did sin they demonstrated brokenness by confessing and accepting grace.

They spoke the truth from the Bible to me by challenging my hypocrisy. I was embarrassed, but thankful and embraced falling in love with Jesus, faithfully and humbly taking ownership and repenting of my sin. I learned things from the Word that I never understood before - salvation issues that clarified why my "Christianity" was so powerless. Grace is in fact not a "get out of Hell free pass" but rather Grace is what teaches me to say "no" to ungodliness and live in the light (Tit 2:12). I had been riddled with shame and regret for four years due to the fact that at 19 I got pregnant and made the even worse decision to have an abortion. We are only as sick as our secrets and I discovered that it only takes one to be in the darkness. Thank God for confession and repentance.

On March 5th 1994, I got baptized, understanding for the first time where and how to become a New Creation. Thanks to Christ's sacrifice, all my sin was forgiven, I received the gift of the Holy Spirit and I was adopted into God's wonderful church family. I saw that being a Disciple of Jesus is about "being the Church" versus simply "going to Church". My journey of growing in **Self Control** over **Spirit, Body and Soul** was officially underway.

> *Acts 2:38 NLT*
> *Peter replied, "Each of you must repent of your sins and turn to God, and be baptized in the name of Jesus Christ for the forgiveness of your sins. Then you will receive the gift of the Holy Spirit.*

I embraced Jesus as my Lord and Savior and was doing my best to walk in step with the Holy Spirit (Gal 5:25). Over the next two decades, as various challenges came my way, I began feeling somewhat victimized by certain emotions - fear, anxiety and bitterness. The cycle of these feelings rendered me episodically "stuck" and increasingly frustrated.

Rather than being "still" and taking the time and focus necessary to mature, I got busier and worked harder. I was like Martha when I needed to be like Mary (Luke 10:38-42). Looking back, I practiced emotional avoidance which robbed my peace (Phil 4:7). I came to realize that some of these uncomfortable feelings were due to current events, while others were triggers from my past. Most of the anxiety I felt was because I allowed my mind to wander into the future, often predicting "worst case scenarios". I did believe, but I failed to renew my nagging intrusive unbelief (Mark 9:24).

Though I cried out to God, studied my Bible, and shared my burdens with fellow Disciples, I lacked sufficient knowledge and application for true transformation. I spent years focused first on growing the church versus growing up spiritually myself and loving others accordingly. I mistook the Great Commission (Matt 28:18-20) for the Greatest Commandments

Me - hoping things get better

14

(Matt 22:36-40). I found myself feeling like a hamster on a wheel - running but going nowhere and becoming increasingly disturbed.

Jesus did not get busier when things got tougher - He slowed down and turned to His Father's loving arms, embracing God's love and then, with this love, poured into others (Luk 5:16). You see, the Great Commission (Matt 28:18-20) happens almost as a by-product when we fill up with God's love first (Matt 22:37-38).

I had unintentionally forsaken my first Love (Rev 2:2-5). As essential as belief in Jesus, repentance and baptism are for salvation, so too is the expectation for maturity (1 Pet 2:2). Sadly many get baptized only to drift and fall away. I had allowed myself to get distracted by "good things" and in so doing I had neglected my responsibility of personal spiritual development.

It was within that environment that the vision for this 3 Part Workbook Series was born and I am honored to share it with you. My heartfelt prayer, dear Reader, is that you will learn from my ignorance, sin and pain. Be inspired to continue to respond to God's call for personal spiritual maturity.   When we do our part in growing by taking control of what dominates our mind and our mood we refuse to be the victim. We learn to rise above events, circumstances and personalities whether past, present or future. With the power of the Holy Spirit we get to renew our minds and revel in the peace that surpasses all understanding (Phil 4:4-9).

Here's to God's beautiful purpose for us: to become a true Disciple of Jesus and then to mature by walking in step with His powerful Holy Spirit (Gal 5:25) - exercising **Self Control** over **Spirit, Body and Soul**.

"The best way to get something done is to begin" - Unknown

Chapter 1

LOVE THE LORD: DEVELOPING SELF CONTROL PART A

WHAT IS SELF CONTROL?

The definition of Self Control according to Thayer's dictionary: the virtue of one who masters his desires and passions, especially his sensual appetites

Another definition according to Oxford Languages: the ability to control oneself, in particular one's emotions and desires or the expression of them in one's behavior, especially in difficult situations.

It is safe to say that every person has room to grow in self control. In fact, any time we sin it is, in essence, a demonstration that we lack self control. God knows this and that is why He sent Jesus to save us by grace. So, we continue to need His mercy and forgiveness after baptism. However, that being said, grace is not to be taken advantage of. We cannot mistake God's kindness for weakness. He expects us to be actively growing in self control. Since God's love language is obedience, we get to encourage God as we mature spiritually.

"Control yourself or someone else will control you." - Unknown

For God will never give you the spirit of fear, but the Holy Spirit who gives you mighty power, love, and self-control. (2 Timothy 1:7 TPT)

Self control gives you the strength to master right thinking which breeds the power of calmness. This pleases God and enables us to live full, fruitful, love based lives.

PATIENCE IS A MARKER OF SELF CONTROL

Better a patient person than a warrior, one with self-control than one who takes a city. (Proverbs 16:32)

God teaches here that patience is a marker of self control. This is personally very convicting to me since patience is something I am constantly needing to focus on developing. I see that this is where I also lack self control. When little things bother me and I become easily annoyed, I consider this a warning sign to pay more attention to my thoughts and feelings. I need to find

> **"Self control is strength. Right thought is mastery. Calmness is power."**
> **- James Allen, author of "As a Man Thinketh" published in 1903**

the root of my "snippy" (disrespectful) attitude. Once I bring it all to mind and often to paper, I am then able to redirect my thoughts back to what pleases the Lord.

Remember, once self controlled, not always self controlled. It is more like your muscles that need repeated strengthening and stretching. In other words, what matters is where we are right now in our choice to practice self control, not how self controlled we were yesterday or last year. We can choose to be disciplined as we allow the Cross to compel us. Jesus should always be and stay our "Why". This disciplined thinking takes intentionality which requires self control.

Reflection:

Q: Do you see your patience as a reflection of your level of self control?

Q: On a scale of 1-10 with 10 being completely self controlled, how do you rate yourself today? Describe why you rated yourself as you did.

BEING SLOW TO SPEAK IS ANOTHER MARKER OF SELF CONTROL

Calming ourselves down in order to be slow to speak in order to be quick to think, is another marker of self control. We must train ourselves to think about what we will say so as to speak in a manner worthy of the Gospel.

> *My dear brothers and sisters, take note of this: Everyone should be quick to listen, slow to speak and slow to become angry. (James 1:19)*

When we think before speaking, we reap many benefits, these are even backed up by scientific evidence. Studies show that when we take time to think before reacting, we engage our prefrontal cortex, which is associated with impulse control, regulating emotional responses and considering potential consequences. This approach thus enhances our ability to problem solve. We are able to consider various perspectives and outcomes. Almost as though we place all our feelings and thoughts into a glass jar and are now able to consider them from multiple perspectives.

This vantage point brings clarity and can be useful to identify deeper meaning, gravity and patterns. We are also able to communicate more simply and reduce misunderstandings. This way we manage our cognitive load, guarding against overload or overwhelm. All this will only be accessible to us if we choose to practice self control over our tongues.

Likewise, the tongue is a small part of the body, but it makes great boasts. Consider what a great forest is set on fire by a small spark. The tongue also is a fire, a world of evil among the parts of the body. It corrupts the whole body, sets the whole course of one's life on fire, and is itself set on fire by hell. All kinds of animals, birds, reptiles and sea creatures are being tamed and have been tamed by mankind, but no human being can tame the tongue. It is a restless evil, full of deadly poison. With the tongue we praise our Lord and Father, and with it we curse human beings, who have been made in God's likeness. Out of the same mouth come praise and cursing. My brothers and sisters, this should not be. (James 3:5-10)

Our thoughts and feelings in a glass jar, ready for analysing

Since we have the Holy Spirit in us, we can and must continue to grow the fruit of self control. Whatever comes out of our mouth is a reflection of what is in our hearts. These thoughts and feelings are what we need to dissect and sometimes reconstruct.

But the things that come out of a person's mouth come from the heart, and these defile them. (Matthew 15:18)

Those who consider themselves religious and yet do not keep a tight rein on their tongues deceive themselves, and their religion is worthless. (James 1:26)

Without self control, our religion is worthless. I will always be grateful for a dear sister who used to advise me to "bite my tongue (until it bleeds if necessary) instead of saying anything in haste". The point she was making is that there is no excuse not to have a tight rein on our tongues.

"Discipline is the bridge between goals and accomplishment." - John Rohn

Reflection:

Q: Are you slow to speak?

Q: What do you regret saying most recently?

Q: Do you tend to cut people off often? If so, why?

SUCCESSFUL PEOPLE ARE SELF CONTROLLED

Every person who has accomplished anything remotely admirable has adopted a disciplined, self controlled mindset. Paul understood the self control necessary for athletes to excel and he uses this example of physical discipline to spur us on spiritually. The rewards that professional athletes aspire to are trophies, titles and money. We are promised a life of purpose greater than self and then Heaven, if we remain faithful! These rewards are eternal and therefore so much more valuable. If what is less valuable requires self control, how much more is the invaluable only achieved by adopting a self controlled mindset in all areas. We must be on our guard as we wage spiritual battles daily while remaining in a state of peacefulness.

Just like we can set a dial or switch, so too we can set our minds.

Every athlete exercises self-control in all things. They do it to receive a perishable wreath, but we an imperishable. Well, I do not run aimlessly, I do not box as one beating the air; but I pommel my body and subdue it, lest after preaching to others I myself should be disqualified. (1 Corinthians 9:25-27 RSV)

Just like setting our alarm clock or a timer is simple and attainable, so too, setting our mind should become simple and attainable. This only happens by strict training of our thinking. This is the hard work that most choose to ignore or neglect.

Set your minds on things above, not on earthly things. (Colossians 3:2)

After all, self control is a fruit of the Spirit so we absolutely have unlimited access to it, if we do our part in being disciplined to practice it.

But the Holy Spirit produces this kind of fruit in our lives: love, joy, peace, patience, kindness, goodness, faithfulness, gentleness, and self-control. There is no law against these things! (Galatians 5:22-23 NLT)

In order to keep in step with the Spirit we must practice self control. To practice is to do what's right consistently, even when you don't feel like it. God does not condone our lack of self control. In fact if we are not growing in this quality we will most likely not make it to heaven. It is our responsibility to know, grow and practice self control!

A wise man once told me: "Character is being where you say you will be, doing what you say you will do and doing it to the best of your ability". As we consider this wisdom we can see that self control has a great deal to do with character building. In fact they are integrally intertwined. Gain self control and you will be building character.

Reflection:

Q: Are you intentional about growing up and maturing spiritually? If so, what are you doing? If not, why?

Q: How often do you do what you do not feel like doing?

Q: List some of the things you do that you do not necessarily feel like doing.

CAIN: A GOOD, BAD EXAMPLE

"Why are you so angry?" the LORD asked Cain. "Why do you look so dejected? You will be accepted if you do what is right. But if you refuse to do what is right, then watch out! Sin is crouching at the door, eager to control you. But you must subdue it and be its master." (Genesis 4:6-7 NLT)

God teaches us about self control from the very beginning. He addresses Cain's anger and depression (dejection). God attempted to draw him out by asking him why he was feeling this way. If Cain had chosen to be respectful and trusting then he would have thought about the question God posed and given Him an honest answer. He would have processed his emotions by tracing them back to his thoughts. His thinking was that God was happier with his brother Abel than with him. Then the discussion about "why" would have happened. Cain might have then "come to his senses" and realized that he made the choice to give God less than his best. He could have appreciated the guilt feeling since it served as a warning sign to pay attention to his sin and repent. His heart would have softened as he became aware of his own sin. He could have apologized to God and to Abel and the narrative would have been radically different. This is how we "subdue" and "master" our sin.

> **"Sin will take you further then you want to go and keep you longer then you want to stay."**
> **- Ravi Zacharias**

Instead, he hardened his heart, remained silent and did not take the Lord's warning seriously. He refused to practice self control by doing what was right, he did not subdue or master his sin but recklessly gave into it and became the world's first murderer.

As shocked as we may be at Cain's lack of self control, technically, anytime we sin, we are demonstrating the same thing.

Reflection:

Q: What can you learn from the questions God asked Cain in Genesis 4 and how can you apply them?

SAMSON - ANOTHER GOOD BAD EXAMPLE

Samson's life was a sad story, riddled with a lack of self control. Though chosen by God to do great things and gifted with incredible physical strength, his lack of self control led to his doom. In Judges 16, Samson refuses to obey God and his parents as he chooses to fall in "lust" with yet another Philistine woman. Disobedience is like the "Kryptonite" to self control. Had Samson fled from temptation, Delilah would not have been able to manipulate him into revealing the source of his power. His lack of self control led to cowering to his sexual desires that ultimately rendered him captive to his Philistine enemies. They gouged out his lustful eyes and reduced him to work like a mule.

What tragic and unnecessary consequences Samson suffered because he refused to learn self control. He was misguided by his lustful thoughts and emotions. Without self control we are all enslaved by our idols.

Unfortunately, I can relate to Samson since I also chose to indulge in gross impurity. I knew it was wrong because I felt ashamed. Rather than confess and gain control over it, I kept it hidden and well fed. This undisciplined mindset led to numerous impure interactions with men. It didn't stop there, at 19 I made the choice to be sexually immoral and soon after I became pregnant. My out-of-control thinking continued and to my shame I chose to abort my baby. I was out of control in my selfish foolishness.

By God's grace I repented before getting baptized and to date continue to tap into the power of God's grace as I say "no" to out of control impure thinking.

> *For the grace of God has appeared that offers salvation to all people. It teaches us to say "No" to ungodliness and worldly passions, and to live self-controlled, upright and godly lives in this present age, (Titus 2:11-12)*

Reflection:

Q: Are you in control of your purity? How about your sobriety?

Q: If not, describe how you feel when you succumb to your cravings?

SELF CONTROL IS A JOURNEY, NOT A DESTINATION

Developing our self control does take time and is a process. It only grows when we are intentional, when we make it a priority. I knew a lot about what the Bible said about things like respecting my husband in everything or not giving in to fear. However, somehow applying these principles consistently felt intangible.

When I first got married, I battled submitting to my wonderful Husband, Chris, because I lacked self control. It is difficult to give up our will and opinion, especially when we feel like our idea makes more sense. Can any wives relate? This is exactly where submission is exercised by the way! It is in fact the choice to surrender our will and opinion to their will and opinion when we do not agree! Otherwise, our husbands are doing what we agree with and there is no submission necessary. Can I get an "Amen" Sisters?

Perhaps you were raised in a household where Mom "wore the pants" more than she should have. Sometimes this happens out of necessity, due to Dad's absence, or out of fear of Dad's incompetence. This is not the plan God designed for marriage. Unfortunately, the "apple doesn't fall far from the tree" and so the children imitate this model that sadly is one lacking in self control. I struggled with fear and pride, which made submitting to Chris a definite challenge for me (nothing against Chris). This was my own baggage I needed to sort through. I needed to develop self control to face the uncomfortable and deal with it.

Later on, when I was blessed with two incredible children. I wrestled a lot with fear. What if they were not healthy or perhaps, I wouldn't be a good Mother. This was when I read an incredible book, "This Doesn't Feel Like Love", by Roger and Marsha Lamb. Their vulnerable and noble testimony helped me to change my perspective. Instead of praying for the child I wanted, I started praying for the child I needed. This helped me practice self control over the pressure I felt during my pregnancies. Even today this mindset helps me to control where I allow my thoughts to go in regards to my wonderful children.

Babies grow up and before your very eyes your innocent little angels transform into moody preteens and rebellious teenagers. Puberty happens to all of us and comes with its set of challenges. On a side note, parents do not allow your son to think "he" should be a "she" or vice versa. Love them, teach them the truth from the Word and be available to them (see more details in chapter 9 on being a Godly Parent). During these stages I struggled again with fear, anxiety, sadness and doubt. Witnessing my obedient children I love so much be overcome by deceit and bad choices was an extremely painful period for me. When we are sensitive to the spiritual battle we understand the reality of this shift, which makes it even more painful.

I always love my fabulous children deeply, but there were days I did not like them! Thankfully I stayed on my knees and had great advisors encouraging me along the way. Wise men and women reminded me that they had to go into the darkness in order to find the light for themselves. I learned that forgiving my children everyday was necessary and that this required self control on my part. It was never a warm fuzzy feeling, rather a decision to do the right thing. I woke up and chose to forgive them, one day at a time. This has and still does guard my heart against getting hurt, bitter, mean and self-righteous.

By the way, my children are amazing and I know their bad choices were not personal. I needed to learn self control to not "take them personally". They were going through the natural process of growing up and finding their own conviction and standards. Chris and I came up with a good acronym we still use today:

Reflection:

Q: How about you? Can you relate? If so, how?

OUT OF CONTROL NEVER TURNS OUT WELL

I remember a sad case of two wonderful singles, let's call them Brad and Carrie. They both changed radically and got baptized while at college. Soon they developed an interest and attraction for each other, which isn't a problem in and of itself. However, rather than practicing self control over their affections and maintain pure boundaries, they crossed emotional lines of intimacy and also deliberately sinned by violating their purity. Their immorality hardened them both towards God and the people around them who advised them to repent. Suddenly they were gone and apparently eloped, severing relationships with so many for the sake of their lack of self control. A sad consequence of division caused by lack of self control.

Another dear sister went back to consistently hanging around her old friend group where she learned to smoke pot. Even though she had been a faithful disciple for several years, her lack of controlling her influencers led to her choice to pick up using again which dragged her away from the light. Your main friend group will influence who you are.

> *Don't be fooled by those who say such things, for "bad company corrupts good character."*
> *Think carefully about what is right, and stop sinning. (1 Corinthians 15:33-34a NLT)*

Another disciple started working extra hours in order to get ahead and before long was no longer committed to obeying God wholeheartedly. Their love for money was taking over their affection for God. He also drifted away since the Bible warns that we cannot serve both God and money.

> *"No one can serve two masters. For you will hate one and love the other; you will be*
> *devoted to one and despise the other. You cannot serve God and be enslaved to money.*
> *(Matthew 6:24 NLT)*

It absolutely takes denying yourself to build self control since it requires doing what's right, rather than what is easiest and feels good. Lacking self control is described as the terrible state of many people in the last days and so the below scripture defines our society today.

> *"But mark this: There will be terrible times in the last days. People will be lovers of*
> *themselves, lovers of money, boastful, proud, abusive, disobedient to their parents,*
> *ungrateful, unholy, without love, unforgiving, slanderous, without self-control, brutal,*
> *not lovers of the good, treacherous, rash, conceited, lovers of pleasure rather than lovers of*
> *God— having a form of godliness but denying its power. Have nothing to do with such*
> *people." (2 Timothy 3:1-5)*

> **"You become what you give your attention to" - Epictetus, an ancient Greek philosopher**

The above quote is very Biblically sound. Unless we control ourselves by loving God first, making sure we view Him accurately and opening our minds and hearts as we deposit sufficient energy and time into our relationship with Him, we are gradually falling away. Self control directs the mind back to whatever pleases God, not what necessarily feels good in the moment. Consider the visual below:

Adverse circumstances with two polar opposite perspectives. It takes self control to focus on what is good.

Reflection:

Q: Which inmate are you prone to be more like and why?

Q: What areas do you lack self control in?

PEACE - THE ACID TEST FOR SELF CONTROL

In God's mercy He loves and accepts us exactly as we are and He also expects us to grow up! As parents we can identify with this. We expect our babies to develop. If they don't, we understand that there is something wrong. The level of self control we choose to practice largely determines our level of spiritual maturity. Unlike chronological aging where we get older simply because "time waits for no man", spiritual maturity develops when we focus on being more self controlled.

If we neglect this responsibility, we become less spiritually mature. A younger person can be spiritually mature, likewise an older person can be very immature spiritually. Maturity develops when we practice the necessary self control to continue to grow up in our salvation and walk in the light accordingly, not just when we age. If we are not intentional about training ourselves to be self controlled, then by default we are going to be undisciplined in our thinking. It is not difficult to discern spiritual growth since the acid test is PEACE.

> *Rejoice in the Lord always. I will say it again: Rejoice! Let your gentleness be evident to all. The Lord is near. Do not be anxious about anything, but in every situation, by prayer and petition, with thanksgiving, present your requests to God. And the peace of God, which transcends all understanding, will guard your hearts and your minds in Christ Jesus. (Philippians 4:4-7)*

Reflection:

Q: Are you at peace most of the time? If so, why? If not, why?

In Summary:

Self control is essential in order to fight the good fight. We develop this quality by growing in the markers of patience, being slow to speak and overall regulating our thinking. Learning from the good, bad examples in the Bible gives us wisdom to follow to help us live the victorious life God promises. Peace is the acid test as to how self controlled we are. Make the right choice.

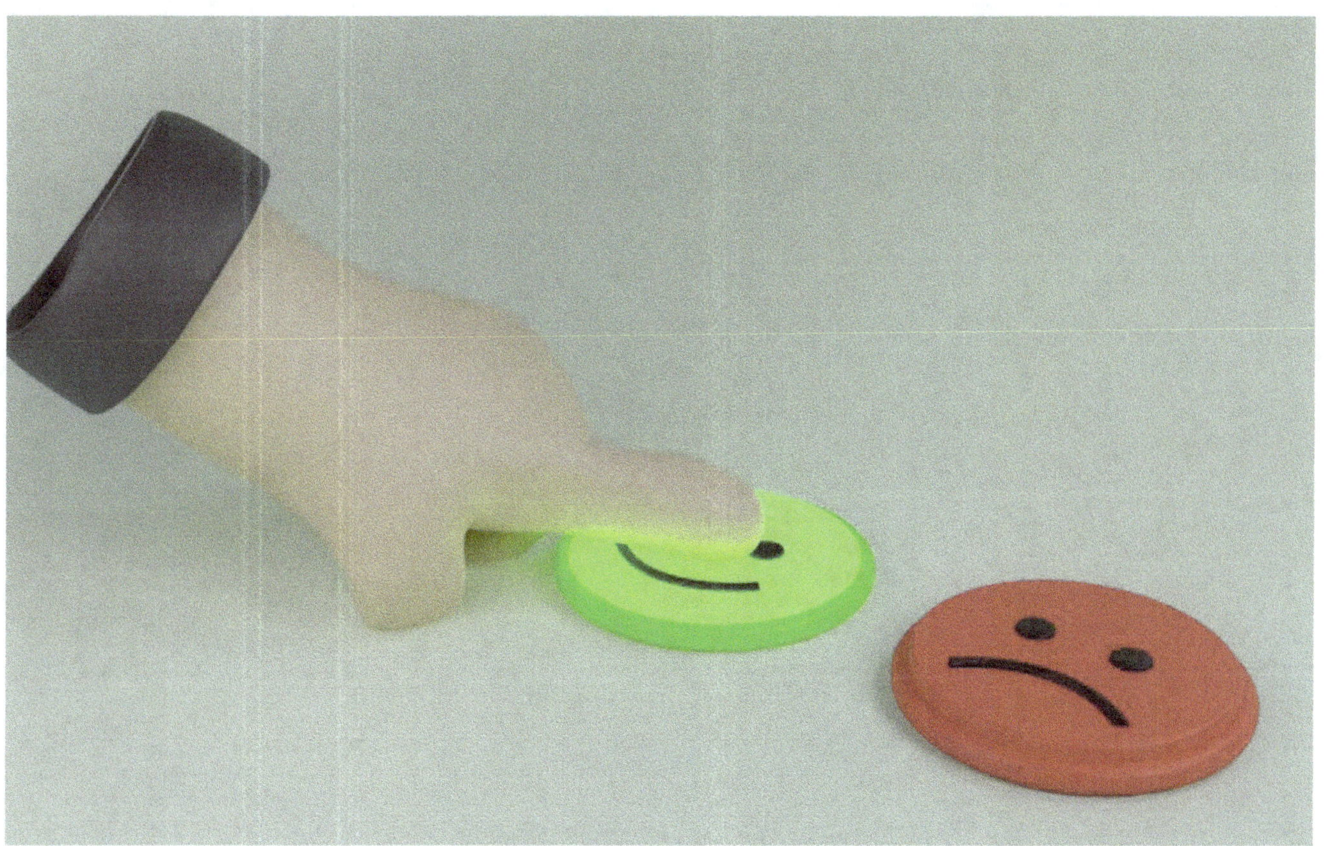

Self control makes the right choice

Chapter 2

LOVE THE LORD: DEVELOPING SELF CONTROL PART B

When we fail to develop self control we become very vulnerable to all kinds of schemes and worldly influences.

LACKING IN SELF CONTROL MAKES US VULNERABLE TO EVIL

A person without self control is like a city with broken-down walls. (Proverbs 25:28 NLT)

Back in Biblical times, a city without walls was very vulnerable to all kinds of dangers, the inhabitants were not safe, and it was only a matter of time until they were violated by bandits or taken captive by some ruthless nation. For us these "walls" today are guarding our hearts and our minds. We must be vigilant and determined, willing to do whatever it takes to keep the walls strong and secure. After we get baptized, we are vulnerable to being sucked back into the world if we do not develop these walls of self control. Loving God first and keeping Him on the throne of our life does not happen unless we make it happen. This takes being constantly regulated and self controlled with our thoughts.

A Vulnerable Place To Be

Guard your heart above all else, for it determines the course of your life. (Proverbs 4:23 NLT)

The quality of your life is determined according to how you guard your heart. If you don't already know this, learn it now! Make this a watershed period where you gain a full understanding of why and how to, above all else, guard your heart. Although I had read this scripture many times, I did not comprehend its significance until I had been a Christian for almost two decades. Instead, I felt out of control at times, almost captive to fear, anxiety or sadness. I allowed my mood to be determined by outside circumstances versus taking the wheel of my mind and controlling myself. It is about controlling where I allow my thoughts to land, not what thoughts pop into my mind. These are largely beyond my control and that's fine if I do my part in not inviting them to move in (or even spend the night!)! The goal is to recognize them as the intruders they are and turn them away at the front door.

WHAT ARE G.N.A.T.S?

When we practice the same out of control negative thinking, over time, they become automatic thought patterns, much like a program in a computer. They are initiated with a simple click. Think about times when something simple has triggered you into a horrible thought circuit and evoked painful emotions and other reactions. These negative automatic thought patterns are what I like to call G.N.A.T.S:

G.N.A.T.S. an acronym for:

G.- GARBAGE .........N.-NEGATIVE......A.-AUTOMATIC.........T.-THOUGHTS.

When we allow intrusive thoughts to dominate our minds, when we do not deal with triggers, when we avoid emotional pain by turning to vices, we multiply our G.N.A.T.S (Garbage Negative Automatic Thoughts). So, we feel overwhelmed and understandably out of control. I picture this chaotic mental and emotional state to look like that of a gnat invasion. This was one of the ten plagues that God sent to get Pharoah's attention. (Exo 8:16-19)

"But when you ask, you must believe and not doubt, because the one who doubts is like a wave of the sea, blown and tossed by the wind. That person should not expect to receive anything from the Lord. Such a person is double-minded and unstable in all they do." (James 1:6-8)

G.N.A.T. Invastion

In the above scripture, the person's G.N.A.T is doubt. They will not receive anything from the Lord and are double-minded and unstable in all they do. They are this way because they have rehearsed doubt instead of faith. This happens easily since we are negatively biased. This term refers to a tendency or predisposition to focus more on negative information, outcomes or experiences than on positive or neutral ones.

After a while of being miserably controlled by negative emotions, I became sick and tired of being sick and tired. Perhaps you can relate? Unfortunately, many of us learn the hard way and need some bad "event" to wake us up. On a side note, it is wiser to learn from others' mistakes than having to suffer the consequences of making them yourself. Anyway, despite my lack of learning this lesson the best way, God had mercy on me and I began to do the work to see that I needed to grow in my self control. I began to see that God expects it and that it is necessary to master in order to conquer my out of control thinking.

I did a lot of research into what thoughts are and discovered many wonderful things. We are thinking beings. Always thinking and these thoughts alter the actual physical structure of our brains. In fact, the physiology of our brain is always changing. Every day we either strengthen the love structures containing our memories or we weaken them by building fear structures instead.

This is so simple, so why are we all not consistently choosing love? The problem is always sin. We all sin and we have all been sinned against. If we sin by neglecting to do the work, then the love influencers weaken. We allow our thinking to veer in the wrong direction, towards fear and chaos. When we do not practice self control over our thoughts and repent quickly, we actually build these toxic structures into our brains which then impact our current and future thinking.

Perhaps you wrestle with Fear, Depression, Anxiety, Anger, Bitterness, Self Righteousness or something else. These feelings are valid and real. Without choosing to develop the self control to actively transform your G.N.A.T.S into what pleases God, you too will reduce yourself to an unstable state.

Reflection:

Q: What are the G.N.A.T.S that you wrestle with the most? List the top three negative thought patterns that dominate your thinking.

Q: Based on the scripture in James 1:6-8, do you see how G.N.A.T.S lead to instability? Do you feel unstable at times? If so, describe these feelings.

There is a reason for the terms accurately describing most people as they age, "bitter old women" and "grumpy old men." We all have G.N.A.T.S and if we do not become deliberate in dealing with them, we too will end up bitter and grumpy.

Reflection:

Q: Are you bitter or grumpy?

BAGGAGE

There is good news. Although we all have G.N.A.T.S, we can all renew our minds and transform them into LOVE BASED THINKING. This is simply the process of practicing a different way of thinking and processing our emotions. This process doesn't happen miraculously by itself, rather it is intentional and bears great transformation from within. Without this focus we will progressively conform to the pattern of the world.

If we take time to think about our thinking with complete honesty, then we can identify what our G.N.A.T.S are. We are saved and forgiven at the waters of baptism; this does not mean that all our baggage gets washed away. We are responsible for renewing this baggage as we mature spiritually. The weight of our baggage is determined by how many G.N.A.T.S we have accumulated. Most, including myself, have even built G.N.A.T.S as a Disciple. What I mean by this is that I was not adequitely regulated with my thoughts for a long time as a Christian and with that came various negative patterns of thought. For example, when faced with certain circumstances I reacted in fear and ended up stuffing and growing fear. Instead I should have faced, processed and landed it in the Love Zone. We transform by rewiring this toxic luggage. To stay saved and mature, mind renewal is essential. God is patient but He does expect progress.

Do You Feel Like This Poor Horse?

Oftentimes we want to treat God like our personal genie since we expect him to deliver us from all pain instantaneously. We can begin to use the scripture like a band aid. This method can only seem to work for a limited time. Our negative thought patterns (G.N.A.T.S) will accumulate and in time will catch up to us.

Every experience we have manifests in three places: in our minds as gravitational fields, in our brains as physical structures and in every one of our cell bodies throughout our bodies. That is also why we have signs from our bodies when we think certain things. Some of the ways the body remembers trauma is by responding as it did during the bad experience. For example, your physical symptoms could be: having sweaty palms, trouble breathing, fidgeting, emotional eating when you aren't physically hungry, heart rate increasing, GI issues, trouble focusing or concentrating, restless sleep, biting nails, etc. If unattended, these G.N.A.T.S will negatively impact your entire being. They are like festering wounds, growing fibroids or cancerous tumors that require special attention and treatment to be healed.

To be healthy and mature spiritually we need to be willing to feel worse, before we feel better. This too requires great self control since nobody wants to feel pain. We get rid of our baggage by responsibly doing the work to renew our minds. Our G.N.A.T.S. can and must be denatured and reconstructed into a love attitude that pleases our God and aligns with His love. (We will explore more specifics on mind renewal in chapters 24 and 25 of Part 3 of this Workook Series). The scripture below teaches us that in order to be transformed we should constantly be renewing our minds.

Do not conform to the pattern of this world, but be transformed by the renewing of your mind. Then you will be able to test and approve what God's will is—his good, pleasing and perfect will. (Romans 12:2)

Reflection:

Q: Do you believe you can renew your G.N.A.T.S? If so, why? If not, why?

WHAT IS THE LOVE ZONE?

Self control is essential to direct and redirect our thinking into the Love Zone. The whole Bible is all about LOVE! You are not remaining in His love unless you are consciously bringing your thinking back to His Love, back to the Love Zone. John tells us to remain in his Love.

"As the Father has loved me, so have I loved you. Now remain in my love." (John 15:9)

We all know that the greatest two commandments are all about loving God first, accepting his love for us and then pouring this love into others. Setting the premise for us always to come back to love, no matter what happens.

"Teacher, which is the greatest commandment in the Law?" Jesus replied: "'Love the Lord your God with all your heart and with all your soul and with all your mind.' This is the first and greatest commandment. And the second is like it: 'Love your neighbor as yourself.' All the Law and the Prophets hang on these two commandments." (Matthew 22:36-40)

God says everything is worthless without love and that love will last forever and never fail.

If I could speak all the languages of earth and of angels, but didn't love others, I would only be a noisy gong or a clanging cymbal. If I had the gift of prophecy, and if I understood all of God's secret plans and possessed all knowledge, and if I had such faith that I could move mountains, but didn't love others, I would be nothing. If I gave everything I have to the poor and even sacrificed my body, I could boast about it; but if I didn't love others, I would have gained nothing. (1 Corinthians 13:1-3)

Prophecy and speaking in unknown languages and special knowledge will become useless. But love will last forever! (1 Corinthians 13:1-3;8 NLT)

There are several descriptions in the Scriptures of how crucial Love Zone thinking is and what exactly it includes. Below are a few of perhaps the main ones:

Love is patient and kind. Love is not jealous or boastful or proud or rude. It does not demand its own way. It is not irritable, and it keeps no record of being wronged. It does not rejoice about injustice but rejoices whenever the truth wins out. Love never gives up, never loses faith, is always hopeful, and endures through every circumstance. (1 Corinthians 13:4-7 NLT)

Do nothing out of selfish ambition or vain conceit. Rather, in humility value others above yourselves, not looking to your own interests but each of you to the interests of the others. In your relationships with one another, have the same mindset as Christ Jesus: Who, being in very nature God, did not consider equality with God something to be used to his own advantage; rather, he made himself nothing by taking the very nature of a servant, being made in human likeness. And being found in appearance as a man, he humbled himself by becoming obedient to death—even death on a cross! (Philippians 2:3-8)

The wicked flee though no one pursues, but the righteous are as bold as a lion. (Proverbs 28:1)

For the grace of God has appeared that offers salvation to all people. It teaches us to say "No" to ungodliness and worldly passions, and to live self controlled, upright and godly lives in this present age, (Titus 2:11-12)

However, do not rejoice that the spirits submit to you, but rejoice that your names are written in heaven." (Luke 10:20)

For the Son of Man came to seek and to save the lost." (Luke 19:10)

But godliness with contentment is great gain. (1 Timothy 6:6)

Rejoice always, pray continually, give thanks in all circumstances; for this is God's will for you in Christ Jesus. (1 Thessalonians 5:16-18)

Be joyful in hope, patient in affliction, faithful in prayer. Share with the Lord's people who are in need. Practice hospitality. (Romans 12:12-13)

"This is how my heavenly Father will treat each of you unless you forgive your brother or sister from your heart." (Matthew 18:35)

But the fruit of the Spirit is love, joy, peace, forbearance, kindness, goodness, faithfulness, gentleness and self control. Against such things there is no law. Those who belong to Christ Jesus have crucified the flesh with its passions and desires. (Galatians 5:22-24)

To the right is a poster I made years ago describing the Love Zone. (Sorry that some qualities are written as adjectives while others as nouns). Prayerfully you get the idea. These are all Love Zone mindsets.

Reflection:

Q: Consider all the qualities of love on the love tree below and search your heart and mind. Do these describe your thoughts and feelings most of the time?

Q: Which three qualities of love are you strongest in?

Q: Which one do you need the most help with?

Q: What is your definition of Love? What is it based on?

SELF CONTROLLED, NOT A VICTIM

All the qualities of love that God describes in his Word are acceptable Love attitudes. How we choose to think will directly impact our feelings. This is remarkable because it proves that we do indeed have control over our emotions by taking control of our thoughts. We are not victims to either our emotions or someone else's choices. As simple and obvious as this truth is, I failed to realize and claim it for too long.

Love Zone Poster

> **"You cannot control what happens to you, but you can control your attitude toward what happens to you, and in that you will be mastering change rather than allowing it to master you."**
> **- Dan Kennedy**

Imagine regulating your thinking so well with such self control, that you become instantly aware of all thoughts that are not love based. You quickly identify them as such, unpack them regardless of the pain associated and then make the necessary changes to steer yourself back to the Love Zone.

If you disciplined yourself to do this no matter what events and circumstances came your way, you would know exactly how to deal with them by bringing your thinking back into the Love Zone. Where we experience the peace that passes all understanding. This is God's will for us, Paul described it well below:

Always be full of joy in the Lord. I say it again-rejoice! Let everyone see that you are considerate in all you do. Remember, the Lord is coming soon. Don't worry about anything; instead, pray about everything. Tell God what you need, and thank him for all he has done. Then you will experience God's peace, which exceeds anything we can understand. His peace will guard your hearts and minds as you live in Christ Jesus. And now, dear brothers and sisters, one final thing. Fix your thoughts on what is true, and honorable, and right, and pure, and lovely, and admirable. Think about things that are excellent and worthy of praise. (Philippians 4:4-8 NLT)

Reflection:

Q: How does the imagery to the right make you feel? Why?

Q: Do you live in the Love Zone most of the time? If not, why?

The Love Zone - That peaceful mindset routed in love

THE CONVEYOR BELT METAPHOR

Picture your mind as your thought factory's conveyor belt and your thoughts being the products produced in your factory. You are the inspector of each product and your job is to stand guard at the conveyor belt of your thinking factory. As you observe your approximate 30,0000 to 60,000 thoughts per day, your responsibility is to inspect each of them for any imperfections. For any "lack of love" defects.

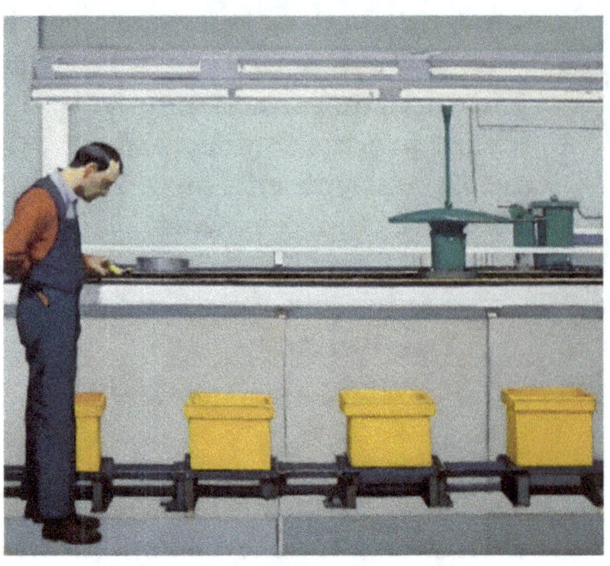

You inspecting your thoughts on your factory's conveyor belt

With all the thoughts (products) that are love based you should smile, ruminate on, revel in and enjoy. While the thoughts that are fear based you must deliberately remove from the belt and work on renewing or restoring them. This is how you take captive every thought. Then you get to make it obedient to Christ. As you practice self-discipline in this way you gain control over your thoughts, feelings and actions. Otherwise, you hurt God, others and yourself.

We demolish arguments and every pretension that sets itself up against the knowledge of God, and we take captive every thought to make it obedient to Christ. (2 Corinthians 10:5)

Our ever growing love relationship with God, thanks to Jesus's sacrifice, is what compels us to be a vigilant, reliable and grateful inspector. Not entitled, greedy or self-piteous. We get to develop self control in increasing measure, and we all need grace along the way.

Prepare your minds for action and exercise self control. Put all your hope in the gracious salvation that will come to you when Jesus Christ is revealed to the world. (1 Peter 1:13 NLT)

Reflection:

Q: Are you aware of what your thoughts are on the conveyor belt of your mind factory?

Q: As your factory's inspector, how is your work ethic and overall attitude?

SELF CONTROL IS TO BE TAKEN SERIOUSLY

Too many disciples are playing with sin by not taking control of their thinking. There are real consequences to lack of self control. Let's see what God says about this deceived mindset:

It should always be only Jesus

For this very reason, make every effort to add to your faith goodness; and to goodness, knowledge; and to knowledge, self control; and to self control, perseverance; and to perseverance, godliness and to godliness, mutual affection; and to mutual affection, love. For if you possess these qualities in increasing measure, they will keep you from being ineffective and unproductive in your knowledge of our Lord Jesus Christ. But whoever does not have them is nearsighted and blind, forgetting that they have been cleansed from their past sins. (2 Peter 1:5-9)

To become nearsighted and blind is when you lose your vision of how wonderful it is to be saved and how God wants to use you. We can then start to lust after the world and become increasingly deceived as to the schemes of the devil. Do not be deceived that Satan's whole goal is to take every true disciple back to the darkness and ultimately to Hell with him. This is his revenge on God.

And there was war in heaven: Michael and his angels fought against the dragon; and the dragon fought and his angels, And prevailed not; neither was their place found any more in heaven. Revelation 12:7-8

Satan is likened to a ferocious lion for a reason

Satan is our enemy and he is prowling around desiring to destroy us. His plot is to destroy us in the battlefield of our minds.

Be watchful and control yourselves. Your enemy the devil is like a roaring lion. He prowls around looking for someone to swallow up. (1 Peter 5:8 NIRV)

A lion's jaw strength is incredibly powerful, their bite force around 1,000 to 1,200 pounds per square inch. This means that crushing a skull comes easily to them.

Reflection:

Q: Do you possess self control in increasing measure?

Q: What areas have you become more self controlled in over the past 6 months?

SELF CONTROL PUTS JESUS IN CONTROL

Appreciating the Cross, making Jesus our Lord and keeping Him as our first Love is not a warm fuzzy feeling. It takes great intentionality and self control on our part.

> *And my God will meet all your needs according to the riches of his glory in Christ Jesus. (Philippians 4:19)*

On the contrary, when we lack this self control, even with the best intentions, we do not get the regular infusions of faith, hope, and love. These fuel us for the spiritual battles we wield internally and externally. Eventually we become so malnourished that we quit even trying. We reduce ourselves to being like a dead cell phone, useless.

Reflection:

Q: Are you inspired to grow in your self control? If so, why? If not, why?

A person without self control

In Summary:

Let us focus on and continue to master self control. All sin stems from a lack of it. When we allow our out of control thoughts and subsequent emotions to dominate our attitude it only causes heartache and misery. Take the time and energy necessary to gain the knowledge on how to have Self Control over your Spirit, Body and Soul, giving God all the glory.

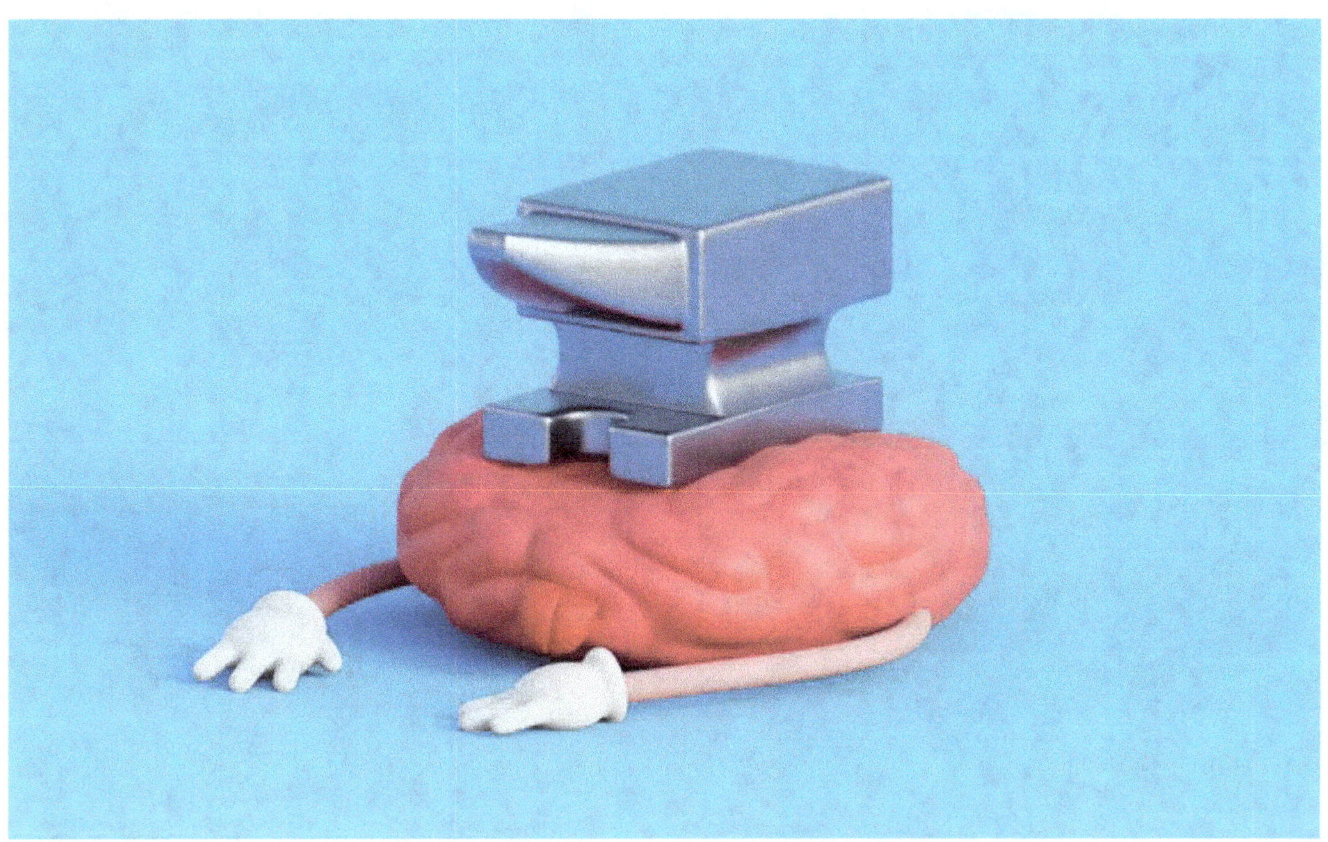

We cannot thrive without self control

Chapter 3

LOVE THE LORD: NOURISH TO FLOURISH

UNDERSTANDING THE HOLY SPIRIT

Have you ever had a houseplant that you took great care of and as a result saw it flourish? Perhaps, like me, you've also had to bury quite a few due to neglect? If you have been around a hungry baby you understand that they make well known when it's time to feed, burp or change their diaper. Anything that is alive needs nourishment, even just to survive. To thrive, the correct dosage of proper nutrients at the appropriate intervals are essential. These are great visuals to relate to nourishing the Holy Spirit that resides within us too.

PRIORITIZE THE INVISIBLE, THE SPIRITUAL

It is easier to pay attention to what is visible and tangible. The invisible and intangible can be readily neglected.

> *For physical training is of some value, but godliness has value for all things, holding promise for both the present life and the life to come. (1 Timothy 4:8)*

In this passage, Paul inspires us to apply the physical training principles of intentionality, diligence, self-denial, consistency and perseverance to how we approach training ourselves spiritually.

Indeed, we are responsible for caring for our physical bodies but without the necessary fueling and cherishing of what is non-physical, spiritual death is imminent.

Godliness is about nourishing the Holy Spirit in us to flourish spiritually. We will never mature and grow up in our salvation if we do not develop this conviction. It is a privilege to pour our attention, time, heart, mind and energy into nourishing our relationship with our God as our first priority.

"Man shall not live on bread alone, but on every word that comes from the mouth of God." - Jesus Christ

Reflection:

Q: Are you more passionate about your physical fitness than your spiritual fitness? If so, how? What will you do to prioritize godliness?

Q: How do you feel about that?

Q: Which plant does your spiritual state resemble?

Q: How does God feel about that?

Nourished versus malnourished

THE GOOD WE SHOULD DO

The beaconing question is why are we not all constantly soaring spiritually? I believe it begins with doing the good we ought to in training ourselves to be godly as our first agenda.

> *If anyone, then, knows the good they ought to do and doesn't do it, it is sin for them. (James 4:17)*

If we fail to do so, our love for God will wane and the influence of the Holy Spirit in us will be quenched. We may be thriving physically as we devote hours per day to our workout and personal grooooming regime but spiritually, we will suffer and ultimately suffocate.

In order to do the good we ought to do effectively we must understand who the Holy Spirit is and how to nurture this relationship. We must also answer our own questions with the Word, always keeping the Cross at the forefront of our thinking. We should value purity of heart the way God does. Consider how David, the man after God's own heart, yearns for Him in the below scripture.

Godliness holds value for all things

> *As the deer pants for streams of water, so my soul pants for you, my God. My soul thirsts for God, for the living God. When can I go and meet with God? (Psalm 42:1-2)*

Clearly our soul needs adequate and sufficient quenching to truly love our God.

Reflection:

Q: Does this describe your attitude towards spending time loving God? If not, why?

Love is an action word

WHO IS THE HOLY SPIRIT AND WHY WE NEED HIM

For a long time as a Disciple I did not really understand who the Holy Spirit was, what He did nor the power available to me once I received Him.

I did understand that to receive the Holy Spirit takes belief in the truth about the Good News of Jesus. As well as an obedient response of repentance and baptism.

> *Peter replied, "Each of you must repent of your sins and turn to God, and be baptized in the name of Jesus Christ for the forgiveness of your sins. Then you will receive the gift of the Holy Spirit. (Acts 2:38 NLT)*

Interestingly, God introduces us to the Holy Spirit in the first chapter of the Bible:

> *In the beginning God created the heavens and the earth. [2] Now the earth was formless and empty, darkness was over the surface of the deep, and the Spirit of God was hovering over the waters. (Genesis 1:1-2)*

As Jesus became the Son of God, God in the flesh, so the Holy Spirit is part of our triune God too. God is the father, God is the Son, Jesus and God is the Holy Spirit. It is incredible to think that God in his infinite wisdom and love for us planned for Jesus to die and shed his precious blood for us. He then generously equips us with His Holy Spirit. This is how God is with us always and how we have unlimited access to Him instantaneously. We have the same power that raised Jesus from the dead in us if we choose to be conscious of Him and do the work to tap into Him. Learning to control our thoughts, feelings and behaviors are optimally done by igniting the power of the Holy Spirit.

He lives in us to give us 24/7 access to Him. We will sin, because we are sinners, however there is no excuse to stay in sin because we have the Holy Spirit. We are saved thanks to Jesus shedding His blood on the Cross and then God lives in us in the form of the Holy Spirit. The Holy Spirit prompts us to be sensitive to what we allow into our mind and how we process it. This is why we need Him so desperately and how He plays a crucial role in our relationship with God.

Paul does a great job describing the power we have immediate access to in the below passage:

Romans 8:5-16 NIrV
So don't live under the control of sin. If you do, you will think about what sin wants. Live under the control of the Holy Spirit. If you do, you will think about what the Spirit wants. [6] The thoughts of a person ruled by sin bring death. But the mind ruled by the Spirit brings life and peace. [7] The mind ruled by the power of sin is at war with God. It does not obey God's law. It can't. [8] Those who are under the power of sin can't please God. [9] But you are not ruled by the power of sin. Instead, the Holy Spirit rules over you. This is true if the Spirit of God lives in you. Anyone who does not have the Spirit of Christ does not belong to Christ. [10] If Christ lives in you, you will live. Though your body will die because of sin, the Spirit gives you life. The Spirit does this because you have been made right with God. [11] The Spirit of the God who raised Jesus from the dead is living in you. So the God who raised Christ from the dead will also give life to your bodies. He will do this because of his Spirit who lives in you. [12] Brothers and sisters, we have a duty. Our duty is not to live under the power of sin. [13] If you live under the power of sin, you will die. But by the Spirit's power you can put to death the sins you commit. Then you will live. [14] Those who are led by the Spirit of God are children of God. [15] The Spirit you received doesn't make you slaves. Otherwise you would live in fear again. Instead, the Holy Spirit you received made you God's adopted child. By the Spirit's power we call God Abba. Abba means Father. [16] The Spirit himself joins with our spirits. Together they tell us that we are God's children.

Most people have heard the analogy of the demon (the flesh) and the angel (the Holy Spirit), who are sitting on our shoulders, whispering into our ears. When we pay attention to and fuel the flesh, we fill our mind and heart with evil and behave accordingly. When we pay attention to and fuel the Holy Spirit, saying "No" to the flesh, we are choosing to fill our minds with the truth and this choice of self control allows us to rise above the flesh to please God and be at peace. So, let's be sure we understand who the Holy Spirit is and be deliberate in how we access His power in us.

Reflection:

Q: Who are you paying more attention to today?

**Demon (flesh) and Angel (Holy Spirit)
Metaphor**

Q: Do you realize that you have access to God thanks to the Holy Spirit He gave you?

Q: How does this make you feel?

In order to better understand and access the power of the Holy Spirit here are 10 of His characteristics:

1. The Holy Spirit is our Counselor and Advocate, leading us in truth: *"And I will ask the Father, and he will give you another Advocate, who will never leave you. He is the Holy Spirit, who leads into all truth. The world cannot receive him, because it isn't looking for him and doesn't recognize him. But you know him, because he lives with you now and later will be in you." (John 14:16-17 NLT)* He advises us always, He is our counselor, our guide, our therapist. The Holy Spirit is described as the one who will guide, teach and empower us in our journey of faith.

Q: Do you embrace the Holy Spirit as your counselor, guide and therapist? If so, how does this affect your maturity spiritually?

2. Thanks to the Holy Spirit we are never alone: Also evident in the above passage is that He will never leave us! Jesus lived with them in person and then after his ascension God's plan was to deposit the gift of the Holy Spirit into us so that we will always have Him with us. Let this sink into your heart. YOU ARE NEVER EVER ALONE AS A TRUE DISCIPLE! Even when you feel alone at times. Remember your feelings are real and valid, but they are not always the truth! Not only is He with us, the Holy Spirit is in us which should emphasize the intimate relationship we get to share.

Q: On a scale of 1-10, with 10 being the most consciously aware and grateful, how much do you appreciate the Holy Spirit in you? How do you show your appreciation?

3. He is our source of Power, Love and Self-Discipline: *"For God has not given us a spirit of fear and timidity, but of power, love, and self-discipline." (2 Timothy 1:7 NLT)* With the Holy Spirit we are not victims to any type of sin or any trauma we have endured. We are not slaves to fear or timidity but instead are able to process any atrocity through mind renewal to where the origin story no longer hurts us in any way. We are able to conquer all sin as we tap into the power and discipline God provides through accessing the Holy Spirit.

Q: Are you giving way to fear and timidity today?

4. He Intercedes and Sanctifies us on our behalf: *"In the same way, the Spirit helps us in our weakness. We do not know what we ought to pray for, but the Spirit himself intercedes for us through wordless groans. And he who searches our hearts knows the mind of the Spirit, because the Spirit intercedes for God's people in accordance with the will of God." (Romans 8:26-27) "But we ought always to thank God for you, brothers and sisters loved by the Lord, because God chose you as first fruits to be saved through the sanctifying work of the Spirit and through belief in the truth." (2 Thessalonians 2:13)* This means that no matter how challenging life gets, we can call on the Holy Spirit to help us. Be real, be honest, keep it simple. Sometimes the best prayer is repetition of "God help me!" We also see that after baptism we will still sin. Not in a willful pattern of sin since this choice will quench the Holy Spirit, but rather as we strive to be Holy we do miss the mark. The sanctification or cleansing for these sins is constantly given by the Spirit in us as we do our best to continue to mature. I love the analogy of being constantly washed clean under a refreshing shower of grace, all the time. Obviously if you choose to remain in a state of willful, deliberate patterns of unrepentant sin, this will change.

The Holy Spirit is so much extra to show God love us

Reflection:

Q: Do you call on the Holy Spirit for help and believe that it is there?

Q: Do you know that you are always completely clean before God because you are always being sanctified by the Holy Spirit? How does the reality that you are make you feel?

5. We are expected to produce the Fruit of the Spirit: *"But the Holy Spirit produces this kind of fruit in our lives: love, joy, peace, patience, kindness, goodness, faithfulness, gentleness, and self control. There is no law against these things! Those who belong to Christ Jesus have nailed the passions and desires of their sinful nature to his cross and crucified them there." (Galatians 5:22-24 NLT)* This passage teaches that our lives should reflect these "fruit" or "qualities" as we continue to say no to sin. This fruit of the Spirit is also part of the evidence that He resides in us. Again, this fruit does not grow without us providing the appropriate nourishment. As we choose to fuel the Spirit, these incredible qualities will be evident in us in increasing measure.

Q: Are these qualities growing in you today? If so, which ones?

6. The Spirit prompts us and teaches us: *"If we live by the [Holy] Spirit, let us also walk by the Spirit. [If by the Holy Spirit we have our life in God, let us go forward walking in line, our conduct controlled by the Spirit.]" (Galatians 5:25 AMPC)* We should therefore be controlled by the Holy Spirit being our governing influencer over our thinking, feelings and behaviors. Our goal as disciples is not just to practice praying and reading our Bibles once a day, indeed our goal is to walk in step with God's Spirit in us all day, everyday for the rest of our lives. We should all be listening to the promptings of that beautiful quiet voice. *"But when the Father sends the Comforter instead of me-and by the Comforter I mean the Holy Spirit-he will teach you much, as well as remind you of everything I myself have told you" John 14:26 TLB.*

Q: Do you calm down often and long enough to hear this voice? Are you humble to his teaching? If so, how do you calm down?

7. The Spirit comforts us: *"Meanwhile, the church had peace throughout Judea, Galilee and Samaria, and grew in strength and numbers." (Acts 9:31 TLB)* The believers learned how to walk in the fear of the Lord and in the comfort of the Holy Spirit. God knows that we will all experience pain and so in his infinite wisdom, He gives us access to himself in the form of the Holy Spirit as our best friend and comforter! This is also taught in John 14:26 above.

Q: When you need soothing, do you turn to the Holy Spirit? Or do you dodge the pain temporarily by numbing out on some sinful vice?

8.   The Spirit seals our salvation: *"And you also were included in Christ when you heard the message of truth, the gospel of your salvation. When you believed, you were marked in him with a seal, the promised Holy Spirit, who is a deposit guaranteeing our inheritance until the redemption of those who are God's possession— to the praise of his glory." (Ephesians 1:13-14 NIV)* The Holy Spirit signifies our belonging to God and assures that if we choose to walk in the light, our inheritance in God's Kingdom is guaranteed.

Q: Do you appreciate this beautiful promise we all have as true disciples? Q: When last did you thank God for the Holy Spirit?

9.   The Spirit brings Freedom: *"Now the Lord is the Spirit, and where the Spirit of the Lord is, there is freedom." (2 Corinthians 3:17)* Here Paul contrasts the freedom from sin, legalism and the constraints of the old covenant, enabling disciples of Jesus to live in accordance with the Spirit's guidance. *Since we live by the Spirit, let us keep in step with the Spirit. (Galatians 5:25)*

Q: Are you living free from legalism as you enjoy walking in step with God's glorious Spirit?

10. The Spirit can leave you: *"Create in me a pure heart, O God, and renew a steadfast spirit within me. Do not cast me from your presence or take your Holy Spirit from me. Restore to me the joy of your salvation and grant me a willing spirit, to sustain me." (Psalm 51:10-12)* Here we see that David gets broken about his sin with Bathsheba. He realizes that the Holy Spirit can be taken from him should he not repent. *"Then Satan entered Judas, called Iscariot, one of the Twelve." (Luke 22:3)* This is an example of the Holy Spirit leaving someone who refused to repent. We know that Satan and the Spirit do not co-exist. Sadly, Judas commits suicide which further demonstrates the Spirit's absence.

Q: Do you entertain sin thinking that the Spirit would never leave you? Describe what that looks like for you.

The way we have access to the same power that raised Jesus from the dead is through active communion with God through the Holy Spirit, thanks to the blood Jesus shed. We have every need completely met because we have the Holy Spirit. God alone is ENOUGH and when we have God inside us, we are ENOUGH! **When we know better, we can do better.**

Reflection:

Q: Were you aware of all these powerful characteristics of the Holy Spirit as well as our responsibility to access them?

Q: Which qualities do you need to pay more attention to?

In the Bible, there are warnings against various negative attitudes and behaviors that can be detrimental to our relationship with the Holy Spirit. Here are a few examples of how the Bible cautions against mistreating or quenching the Holy Spirit:

Never stop nourishing the Holy Spirit in you

HURTING THE HOLY SPIRIT - WHAT NOT TO DO

1. Blasphemy against the Holy Spirit: Jesus warns about blasphemy against the Holy Spirit, saying, *"And so I tell you, every kind of sin and slander can be forgiven, but blasphemy against the Spirit will not be forgiven." (Matthew 12:31-32)* This emphasizes the seriousness of rejecting the work of the Holy Spirit's Prompting by refusing to repent. Please note that blaspheming the Holy Spirit is not one particular sin, it is rather the failure to adopt a Godly sorrow towards our sin and refuse to repent.

2. Quenching the Spirit: *"Do not quench the Spirit." (1 Thessalonians 5:19)* This verse warns against stifling or suppressing the work of the Holy Spirit in our lives through disobedience, unbelief, or neglect.

3. Grieving the Spirit: *"And do not grieve the Holy Spirit of God, with whom you were sealed for the day of redemption." (Ephesians 4:30)* This verse highlights the danger of causing sorrow or sadness to the Holy Spirit through sinful actions, attitudes, or words.

4. Resisting the Spirit: *"You stiff-necked people! Your hearts and ears are still uncircumcised. You are just like your ancestors: You always resist the Holy Spirit!" (Acts 7:51 NLT)* This verse warns against stubbornly rejecting or resisting the guidance and conviction of the Holy Spirit.

There are consequences to resisting the Holy Spirit

I remember about 10 years into our marriage when we were going through a turbulent time. We had moved states, changed careers, had two busy toddlers, were fostering a precious one year old and remodeling our home. There had also been a huge upheaval in our church family that was very painful. Looking back, I can see how I became guilty of quenching the Holy Spirit's power in me. I was critical and angry towards my dear Husband and started focusing too much on him instead of dealing with my own wicked self-righteous heart. I felt so frustrated and overwhelmed. There were so many unknowns in our lives, and I looked for stability in the waves versus looking up to God enough during the storm.

Thankfully through lots of prayer walks, studying my Bible, crying when I needed to, journaling and confessing my sin to God and others I remember coming to my senses and making a watershed decision. I took my eyes off people and circumstances and put all my energy into focusing back on God, my Great Provider. I revisited what Jesus' sacrifice at the Cross meant to me and got broken and grateful again. I sang to God (even though I can't really sing) often and found my peace by landing in the Love Zone. I chose to trust that God is always a good God and is constantly working for my good. He was in control of the storm, and I needed to surrender. This changed my attitude radically and I got back to enjoying my priceless relationship with God, regardless of the circumstances and people's choices surrounding me. (Of course I apologized to Chris and our children too).

It is so evident that sin of all degrees hinders the work of empowerment in us. By heeding these warnings from the Bible, we as disciples should be encouraged to honor and respect the presence of the Holy Spirit in our lives, to remain attentive to His leading, and to avoid attitudes and actions that restrict the work of the Spirit. It is essential to nourish a healthy relationship of reverence, obedience, and openness with the Holy Spirit to flourish.

Reflection:
Q: Are you in any way quenching the Holy Spirit's power in you? If so, how?

NOURISHING THE HOLY SPIRIT - 3 PRACTICALS:

Being intentional about nourishing the Holy Spirit is essential to flourish.

1. **Foster your relationship with God by learning to pray continually:** *"Rejoice always, pray continually, give thanks in all circumstances; for this is God's will for you in Christ Jesus." (1 Thessalonians 5:16-18)* This describes a mindset of constant awareness of God's presence in me and therefore with me. One way to do this is to connect your breath to God's name "Yahweh." Do this by taking moments throughout your day to become intentional with your breathing. As you know, this is a very effective way to calm down in the moment. However, even more empowering is when we deliberately inhale, we proclaim the beginning of Yahweh so we say "Yah" and when we exhale we proclaim the second syllable of Yahweh, which is "Weh." Try it now, close your eyes and inhale deeply vocalizing "YAH," now exhale rigorously saying "WEH." Make your exhale twice as long as your inhale. Repeat this 10 times and as you do, think about who God is to you and how you appreciate, love and trust Him, no matter what. Do this often throughout your day and see yourself more alert and encouraged as your faith in God's presence within you increases.

2. **Be a diligent student of the Word:** Learn to be still, have a plan, study and journal connecting the principles with practicals that apply to you today. I love to write my prayers down and to then go back and elaborate. This tool helps me to get to what lies behind my anguish. Always stay grounded in the greatest two commandments: *"Jesus replied: 'Love the Lord your God with all your heart and with all your soul and with all your mind.' This is the first and greatest commandment. And the second is like it: 'Love your neighbor as yourself.' All the Law and the Prophets hang on these two commandments." (Matthew 22:37-40)* I always come back to how much God loves me and then how I get to receive his love and pour it into those around me. This model puts all the stress on God, the only One that can handle it. Otherwise, I can be legalistic.

3. **Stay in the Light:** *"If we confess our sins, he is faithful and just and will forgive us our sins and purify us from all unrighteousness. If we claim we have not sinned, we make him out to be a liar and his word is not in us." (1 John 1:9-10)* If you want to be forgiven, confess your sins to God. If you want to grow, mature and change, confess your sin to like-minded people who will pray for you and hold you accountable. Do not go to bed without making right anything that you had a part in that went badly today. When we "mess" up, we get to "fess" up!

Gain your own deep convictions about nourishing the Holy Spirit in you in order to flourish. Any head knowledge you gain must become and remain your heart's passion.

In Summary:

Never underestimate nurturing the Holy Spirit in you. When you apply yourself to understand who He is and practice the power available to you through Him, then you will mature spiritually. You will transform because you believe and act accordingly. Embrace that the Holy Spirit resides in you and is your Counselor, always with you, your source of power, love and self control. He prompts and teaches you, expecting you to bear the fruit of the Spirit. He comforts you, seals your salvation and brings you unlimited freedom.

Be careful never to blaspheme, resist, quench or grieve the Holy Spirit in you. Instead foster your relationship with God as your first priority with prayer, meditation, diligent studying of the Word and consistent confession. Do not allow any darkness to stay. Subsequently you will be equipped to accept His love for you. Then and only then are you equipped to pour this beautiful love into others. If you don't, then you won't. It is that simple.

Unlimited power through the Holy Spirit

Chapter 4

LOVE THE LORD: AVOID THE LOVE BUSTERS

Amazingly we get to make the decision to love God first when we decide to be serious about seeking Him with all our hearts. Becoming a true disciple of Jesus is by far the best and most important decision anyone could ever make. Rather than it being a "one and done" choice, we get to decide everyday for the rest of our lives to keep loving the Lord first, or not.

AMAZING SALVATION

The discipline of nourishing our love for Him is a lifelong privilege and journey if we choose to have a willing and obedient heart.

Isaiah 1:18-20 TPT
Come now and let's deliberate over the next steps to take together." YAHWEH promises you over and over: "Though your sins stain you like scarlet, I will whiten them like bright, new-fallen snow! Even though they are deep red like crimson, they will be made white like wool! [19] If you have a willing heart to let me help you, and if you will obey me, you will feast on the blessings of an abundant harvest.

Willing and obedient

Reflection:

Q: How did you feel the day you made Jesus Lord of your life and got baptized?

THE PARABLE OF THE DIFFERENT HEARTS:

However, along the way, we can drift, get distracted, divided, disillusioned, damaged, deceitful, disrupted, disappointed or even destroyed. We can compromise and get derailed by the schemes of the devil and our own sinful choices. We get hurt in the Church or by someone else and refuse to forgive. We can become enticed again by the "shiny stuff" in the world. This is when our devotion to God and His Church wanes and our once clear vision is blurred. Fueled by our stubbornness and other pride we refuse to obey as we once did.

Isaiah 1:20 But if you are stubborn and refuse to obey, the sword will eat you instead."
The mouth of YAHWEH has spoken.

BE CAREFUL

God warns us about three conditions of the heart that lead to spiritual death.

1. The Hard Heart - On the path
2. The Shallow Heart - On the rocks
3. The Worldly Heart - Among the thorns

The Hard, Shallow and Worldly Heart

Matthew 13:3-8,18-23 NIV
Then he told them many things in parables, saying: "A farmer went out to sow his seed. [4] As he was scattering the seed, some fell along the path, and the birds came and ate it up. [5] Some fell on rocky places, where it did not have much soil. It sprang up quickly, because the soil was shallow. [6] But when the sun came up, the plants were scorched, and they withered because they had no root. [7] Other seed fell among thorns, which grew up and choked the plants. [8] Still other seed fell on good soil, where it produced a crop—a hundred, sixty or thirty times what was sown.

[18] "Listen then to what the parable of the sower means: [19] When anyone hears the message about the kingdom and does not understand it, the evil one comes and snatches away what was sown in their heart. This is the seed sown along the path. [20] The seed falling on rocky ground refers to someone who hears the word and at once receives it with joy. [21] But since they have no root, they last only a short time. When trouble or persecution comes because of the word, they quickly fall away. [22] The seed falling among the thorns refers to someone who hears the word, but the worries of this life and the deceitfulness of wealth choke the word, making it unfruitful. [23] But the seed falling on good soil refers to someone who hears the word and understands it. This is the one who produces a crop, yielding a hundred, sixty or thirty times what was sown."

1. THE HARD HEART ON THE PATH:

This person doesn't build and choose faith in God. They do not spend the time in the Word they need, and they do not open their mind and heart to allow the Word to soften their hearts. Instead, they allow the deception of other "gods" to rob their attention and their affection. People use excuses like: "I'm too busy" or "I believe in what I was taught as a child" or "I don't have to obey God to get to Heaven" or "If God is so good, why is there so much wickedness in this world" or an all-time classic, "I do not believe in organized religion". The latter is fueled by all the corruption in so much of "Christendom" today, so is understandable, but still not an excuse to believe God's plan for His Church. This is another scheme, why not foster a "form of godliness" but take away the power (2 Tim 3:1-5). Of course there are other excuses too, but whatever the reason, this person is not choosing faith in God and His Word. Their heart's will remain hard.

2. THE SHALLOW HEART ON THE ROCKS:

This person chooses to believe in God and His Word in the beginning but does not do what it takes to nourish the Holy Spirit in them to mature spiritually. They at best have a transactional relationship with God and when life gets tough or their faith gets challenged they fall away. Shallow roots, shallow heart. No real deep convictions and willingness to suffer for the Cross. They are looking for a trouble free, easy life. They are takers instead of givers. Their eyes are on the created instead of the Creator. They do not do the work to grow up spiritually and as a result are weak, an easy target since they do not diligently put on their full armor (Eph 6:10-18).

3. THE WORLDLY HEART AMONG THE THORNS:

This person meditates on what is wrong (worries) versus on the truth in the Word. Their love for money and the things of this world chokes out their love for God. They get distracted and deceived, choosing to chase after the wind (Ecc 1:14-17). They resort back to their vomit (Prov 26:11).

Notice how only the seed that was sown on the good soil flourishes. This means one out of four of the seeds perish. Make no mistake, the road is narrow.

> *Matthew 7:13-14 NLT*
> *"You can enter God's Kingdom only through the narrow gate. The highway to hell is broad, and its gate is wide for the many who choose that way. [14] But the gateway to life is very narrow and the road is difficult, and only a few ever find it.*

We are not victims to our nature (DNA) or our nurture (where and how we were raised). Instead, we have the power to choose to do the work to direct our minds and hearts to be the good soil.

Reflection:

Q: What is the current state of your heart? Why?

CHOOSING TO BE THE GOOD HEART:

To avoid being the hard, shallow or worldly heart we need to remember that Satan is the father of lies and that he works in lies, excuses and schemes to lure us away from God. Learning to recognize these wicked scams or "love busters" is the first step to choosing to avoid them.

Ephesians 6:11 NIV
Put on the full armor of God, so that you can take your stand against the devil's schemes.

I have noticed over more than a three decade span that there are basically five "love busters" that seem to be the main reasons why people stop loving God as they could and should. These are schemes we need to expose and conquer in order not to fall away.

THE FIVE MAIN LOVE BUSTERS:

1. Lack of self control in consistent quality time spent:

When I have failed to spend regular time with God daily, I have lacked self control by allowing life to get in my way. Essentially I choose not to spend adequate quality time with God as my first priority. Remember that our goal as followers of Jesus is not just to have a quiet time with God daily but rather to learn to walk with God by being aware of his presence with us, all the time. When we don't allow ourselves the time and space to be still and listen to the Words of God, we become like a dying cell phone. Less and less connected, weaker, weary and lacking in the fruit of the Spirit. In time, if we allow this to become a pattern we will return to the shiny stuff around us and allow it to recapture the place of lordship in our hearts. We justify hitting snooze instead of getting up earlier and we make excuses for why we just do not have enough time or energy. The flesh conflicts with the Spirit and if we fail to nourish the Spirit consistently, it will not flourish and therefore will not have the dominant influence over our thinking which is essential for spiritual development. Please note that there are various degrees of drifting and falling away from God which all happen subtly so we must be vigilant.

Galatians 5:17 NLT
The sinful nature wants to do evil, which is just the opposite of what the Spirit wants. And
the Spirit gives us desires that are the opposite of what the sinful nature desires.

These two forces are constantly fighting each other, so you are not free to carry out your good intentions.

Reflection:

Q: Do you snack on scripture when you "have time" and expect God to be your personal genie, using the Word as a band aid and then wonder why you are stuck?

Be consistant and deliberate

Q: What pattern do you see in terms of your consistency with spending quality time with God and developing your awareness of God's presence with you?

2. Legalism:

I like "To Do Lists" because I feel a sense of order, accomplishment and progress. This method of working is effective for millions. However, if we transfer a "To Do List" mindset into our relationships with God, we reduce him to a mere task. This is disrespectful, legalistic and self righteous. Many disciples believe consciously or subconsciously that God is only pleased with them if they meet a certain quantity and frequency criteria. Interestingly, they make these up themselves or they fall into the trap of thinking that someone can tell them how long to pray, read the Word, how much to give and how often to share the good news. The lie of never skipping a day or God will be mad at you, is "truth" to many. I struggled with this scheme as a young Christian. I wanted to please God and I allowed my and others legalism to dictate what that looked like for me. I am so thankful for my wonderful husband, Chris, who has helped me overcome this "love buster" and enjoy the freedom of walking with God all day long. This goes way beyond "having my quiet time".

> *Matthew 5:8 NLT*
> *God blesses those whose hearts are pure, for they will see God.*

Rather than treating God as something that we need to check off our list in order to be in His good graces, our focus should be on growing our relationship with God with a pure heart. Simply because we love, appreciate and need him. He does not condemn us for "missing a quiet time", "not praying enough" or "messing up again". Instead, He gives us mercy and teaches us humility. Legalism often stems from the desire to be in control and prove ourselves to people. Legalism lacks trust. It is prideful when we do not continuously connect with our God since we are saying that we do not need him.

Have you or I ever been exactly where we are right now? No! We have never been this precise age, had these specific issues, had kids in this literal stage, etc. so why do we think we do not need the wisdom and strength that comes from our God? He does not want a transactional relationship with us. He doesn't condemn us and so we shouldn't condemn ourselves or others. Prayer, special time with God and striving not to sin deliberately is all necessary, however, choosing to love and walk with Him as our best and most treasured relationship is what God desires. This produces purity of heart and mind. There is a sinful shift that happens if we go from desiring to walk with God all day, to needing to earn his love and approval by being dutiful. Much like the prodigal son's older brother (Luke 15:28-32).

Another form of legalism happens when leaders think they have the authority to bind "heavy loads that are hard to carry" around people's necks. Being authoritarian and militant. Ordering them in the name of total commitment and sacrifice to produce mandated numbers of people reached out to and monies expected to be given.

> *Matthew 23:4a NIV*
> *They tie up heavy loads that are hard to carry. Then they put them on other people's shoulders.*

What busts the love that we are supposed to have for one another with this type of wicked behavior is a lack of trust in God and the Disciples. We know from 1 Cor 13 that love always trusts. Instead there is selfish ambition to look good in front of people and to get promoted based on their ability to produce new people and money within a specified time. Manipulation by presenting "half of the picture" becomes part of this sinful legalistic mindset. How often do you hear someone talking about their ministry growth and including how many they had fallen away? More importantly what they are doing to help the disciples to mature and build solid foundations. Keeping people on the roster to be able to count them in their weekly reports. Spending money frivolously while many of their flock live hand to mouth. This hired hand leader is not to be tolerated in God's church. Favoritism and sentimentality can so easily slip into the Church also. Are we to tolerate our standards being lower than those in the world? Are we to turn a blind eye when anyone breaks the law, let alone a leader? Will leaders not be held to a higher standard of judgement? We all need checks and balances.

> *James 3:1 TPT*
> *My dear brothers and sisters don't be so eager to become a teacher in the church since you know that we who teach are held to a higher standard of judgment.*

Toleration and minimization of sin is not grace, but rather favoritism and a lack of righteousness. Legalism is more concerned with attaining certain results within set time frames than it is with upholding the Holiness of God's Church. Does the Bible not say that without holiness, nobody will see God (Heb 12:14)? Everyone has freedom in Christ. You must place yourself under Godly leadership that does not make you stumble. By the way, Jesus never referred to himself as a leader, rather a servant. When the focus is on leadership and production instead of love, purity of heart and servitude, legalism and toxicity flourish.

Reflection:

Q: What are the intentions and motives in your mind and heart towards your relationship with God?

Q: Do you hide God's Word in your heart and meditate on Him all day regardless of whether you've had a quiet time or not?

Q: Are you a legalistic leader or a member being harshly treated? Both will bust your love for God.

I sincerely apologize to anyone if I was ever legalistic or lacking in trust in any way. Please forgive me and feel free to contact me if you'd like to discuss details. I want to own anything I have said or done that hasn't been love based.

3. Failing to have a healthy perspective on who God is:

As a young disciple I struggled to accept God's grace and in turn I also battled to extend grace readily to others. My view of God was gravely distorted and subsequently I often felt insecure and insufficient in my relationship with Him and others. I was raised with the perspective that God is the Judge, Hell is real and that we are punished for sinful behavior. While this is true, God is also filled with unconditional love, grace and mercy. Since my mindset towards God was not balanced by the whole truth, I had a warped perspective of my Father. I was angry when I sinned because I felt like God was mad at me and I felt ashamed. We need to have a healthy view of who God is, not Grace heavy or Judgment heavy, but rather the perfect combination of the two.

> *Ephesians 2:8-9 NLT*
> *God saved you by his grace when you believed. And you can't take credit for this; it is a gift from God. [9] Salvation is not a reward for the good things we have done, so none of us can boast about it.*

> *Ecclesiastes 12:14 NIV*
> *For God will bring every deed into judgment, including every hidden thing, whether it is good or evil.*

I felt like a hamster on a spinning wheel in that no matter how hard I worked, I just wasn't good enough for God to love me. I was trying to earn God's love without even realizing I was doing this. It wasn't until I read two of Jerry Bridges books, "The Pursuit of Holiness" and "The Practice of Godliness" that I realized I had an imbalanced view of God. The solution for me was to spend more time realizing and meditating on

God's grace towards me as I continued to do my best not to sin willfully. I needed to bring my perspective of God into a place of homeostasis by growing my convictions about God's mercy, grace and unconditional love. This helped me adjust my focus and develop my relationship with my God. I now know He is the perfect combination of Judge and Savior. I no longer have to prove myself to Him. I do my best and since I am good enough for Jesus to die for, I know I am good enough!

God is 1000% trustworthy 1000% of the time

Were you raised with deep convictions about how gracious God is, viewing Him as a kind, forgiving Grandfather who does not hold you accountable because he loves you too much? Or were you raised with the emphasis on Judgment and Hell, like I was? Both views of God lack the balance of God's incredible grace as well as His unwavering judgement. Failure to rewire your thinking to create the healthy paradigm will in time result in your love for God being busted.

Reflection:

Q: How do you view God?

Q: Are you grace heavy or judgment heavy? Why?

4. Our relationships with our Physical Fathers:

Our relationship with and view of our physical Fathers and Mothers can also play a big part in how we perceive God. God created parents to be anchors to their children: loving, protecting, teaching and providing for them.

Tragically so many have been abandoned, neglected or otherwise abused by their parents, which often breeds a lack of trust, fear, anger, bitterness and more. Prompted by the agony of this lacking parental love we can also hesitate to trust God as our Father. This makes sense since we have been so disappointed by the idea of a wonderful Father and what that looks and feels like. This mindset is common and totally understandable. It is imperative to examine these relationships, feeling the pain and then rewiring our view on God as our perfect Father. We may need to set new boundaries and adopt other healthy tools in our quest to change our paradigm. We will discuss in detail how to break down toxic thought patterns and rebuild healthy love-based views in the chapters on mind renewal.

Safe, loved, accepted, belonging and abundandtly provided for

VS

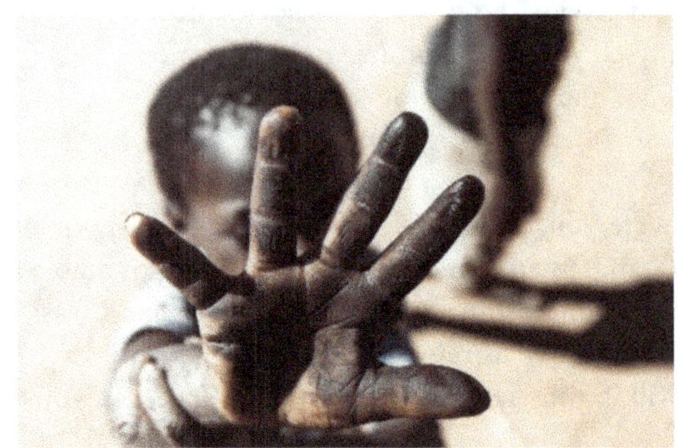

Vulnerable, discarded, rejected, desperate and abandoned

Since our Father God proves his faithful unconditional love to us on the Cross, He is not our flawed, abusive and/or absent physical Father.

Matthew 7:9-11 NIrV
"Suppose your son asks for bread. Which of you will give him a stone? [10] Or suppose he asks for a fish. Which of you will give him a snake? [11] Even though you are evil, you know how to give good gifts to your children. How much more will your Father who is in heaven give good gifts to those who ask him!

God states here that earthly parents are evil and He promises to be faithful and reliable as our Heavenly Father.

In the 2022 study performed by the National Children's Alliance, 76% of child abuse perpetrators were parents or legal guardians and 16% of alleged abusers were themselves children. Tragically oftentimes those who were abused, become abusers. The reality of how many adults struggle with low self-esteem and abandonment issues stems from neglect being the most common form of child abuse. Globally, roughly 1 in 8 girls and 1 in 11 boys have experienced sexual abuse before age 18. Most offenders are known to the child. The trauma that develops here is significant. Learning how to renew our minds from this toxic influence is essential to overcome. We can and must not allow abusive authority figures to bust our love for God.

Reflection:

Q: What perspective do you have towards your physical Father and/or Mother?

Q: How does this perspective influence how you view your Father God?

5. Being in a pattern of willful deliberate sin:

It is true that you are only as sick as your secrets. As we studied the Bible to learn how to become a baptized disciple we all took inventory of our minds and hearts. We chose to believe and made the necessary confessions as we repented. Time marches on after our baptism and we are faced with the privilege of staying in the light by continuing to be honest and open with God about our sin.

> *1 John 1:5-10 NIV*
> *This is the message we have heard from him and declare to you: God is light; in him there is no darkness at all. [6] If we claim to have fellowship with him and yet walk in the darkness, we lie and do not live out the truth. [7] But if we walk in the light, as he is in the light, we have fellowship with one another, and the blood of Jesus, his Son, purifies us from all sin. [8] If we claim to be without sin, we deceive ourselves and the truth is not in us. [9] If we confess our sins, he is faithful and just and will forgive us our sins and purify us from all unrighteousness. [10] If we claim we have not sinned, we make him out to be a liar and his word is not in us.*

We also get to confess to each other to pray for each other. If you want to get forgiven, confess your sin to God. If you really want to change, confess to a fellow disciple who will pray for you and hold you accountable.

> *James 5:16 NIV*
> *Therefore, confess your sins to each other and pray for each other so that you may be healed. The prayer of a righteous person is powerful and effective.*

If we choose not to be transparent we are simply storing secrets again and make no mistake, God will not be mocked. He is not interested in compromising His holiness. It is one thing to be wrestling and doing your best not to sin and still sinning sometimes since this is why Jesus died for us and why we are saved by grace. However, it is another issue if we lose regard for the holiness of our God and return to a lifestyle of blatant rebellion.

Deliberate willful sin enslaves

Hebrews 10:26-31 NLT
Dear friends, if we deliberately continue sinning after we have received knowledge of the truth, there is no longer any sacrifice that will cover these sins. [27] There is only the terrible expectation of God's judgment and the raging fire that will consume his enemies. [28] For anyone who refused to obey the law of Moses was put to death without mercy on the testimony of two or three witnesses. [29] Just think how much worse the punishment will be for those who have trampled on the Son of God, and have treated the blood of the covenant, which made us holy, as if it were common and unholy, and have insulted and disdained the Holy Spirit who brings God's mercy to us. [30] For we know the one who said, "I will take revenge. I will pay them back." He also said, "The LORD will judge his own people." [31] It is a terrible thing to fall into the hands of the living God.

I remember a young woman who I will name Ally, for the sake of her anonymity. She was zealous for many years and strove to love God, people and herself. However, she did not yield to the continued warnings to deal with her past pain. Instead, she disassociated herself and turned to rampant impurity. Her choice to deliberately continue to sin pulled her back into a lifestyle of apathy and purposelessness at best.

Another beautiful Sister, after being faithful to God and his Church for many years, succumbed to her desire to have a boyfriend. She found a tall, dark handsome man and crossed boundaries with him willfully. She took matters into her own hands and did it her way. Needless to say, she was no longer a vibrant force of love for God and others anymore. A man became her idol as she took her eyes off Jesus.

Walking with God and being engaged in a pattern of deliberate willful sin do not mix. Initially, you may feel wonderful. Free from any restrictions. Do not be surprised, if you choose a disobedient lifestyle again, that long term, you will not be free.

Sin so easily entangles us again if we allow it to

Proverbs 28:13-14 NIV
Whoever conceals their sins does not prosper, but the one who confesses and renounces them finds mercy. [14] Blessed is the one who always trembles before God, but whoever hardens their heart falls into trouble.

Miraculously in His mercy, if we want to repent, we can by simply doing what we did at first. Getting back to the basics of making Jesus our number one relationship. As we do so, our disdain for the sin we are wrestling will reappear. We will regain our appreciation for the Grace at the Cross and it will again compel us to say "no" to ungodly patterns.

Revelation 2:5 NLT
Look how far you have fallen! Turn back to me and do the works you did at first. If you don't repent, I will come and remove your lampstand from its place among the churches.

Titus 2:11-14 NIV
For the grace of God has appeared that offers salvation to all people. [12] It teaches us to say "No" to ungodliness and worldly passions, and to live self controlled, upright and godly lives in this present age, [13] while we wait for the blessed hope—the appearing of the glory of our great God and Savior, Jesus Christ, [14] who gave himself for us to redeem us from all wickedness and to purify for himself a people that are his very own, eager to do what is good.

Reflection:

Q: Do you have any secrets today? If so, will you do the right thing to love God?

Examine carefully where your mind and heart are and be humble and urgent to take a deep dive and renew your mind (see chapters 24 and 25 in Part 3 of this Workbook Series), repenting accordingly. Remain aware of the things that can so easily "bust" your love for God and resist them swiftly. If you do not charge your cell phone it will be dead and useless. God is light, He is our source of energy. Stay plugged into Him and He will light us up and work through us in countless ways. God will allow us to blossom and live the full, peaceful and fruitful life He promises.

In Summary:

God says when we choose to be willing and obedient, we flourish. When we allow things and people to "bust" our love for Him we become stubborn and disobedient. Let's be the noble men and women of God by avoiding all the schemes that can become love busters as we deal with our minds and hearts accordingly.

Chapter 5

LOVE THE LORD: UNDERSTANDING GOD IS OMNIPOTENT, OMNISCIENT, AND OMNIPRESENT

After getting baptized it seemed unimaginable to ever lose my awe of God along with the overflowing gratitude I had for Jesus' sacrifice on the Cross. My heart was childlike - soft and pure towards Jesus and His Kingdom. I just felt so thankful to be walking in the light, now saved and part of His incredible family. Despite all my sin, I was free and forgiven, I had a purpose greater than self and my vision was filled with faith, hope and love.

Then one day I struggled with and gave into impurity. I felt shame, regret, fear and anger. I thought about why and how Jesus died and then I allowed myself to be compelled by God's love for me again. I remembered how absolutely awesome He was and how patterns of unconfessed sin can again separate me from the new life I had embraced. Despite being tempted to shut down and isolate, I cried out humbly to God. I wanted prayer and accoutability on my purity so I met with a fellow Christian and made the difficult decision to be open, without minimizing my sin.

The beautiful heart of a child

James 5:16 NIrV
So confess your sins to one another. Pray for one another so that you might be healed. The prayer of a godly person is powerful. Things happen because of it.

Since this is God's way to deal with sin and be healed, my guilt was lifted and I felt the refreshment that comes with repentance. My desire to know God deepened as I was learning more about staying saved thanks to His amazing grace. I learned from this bad choice and came up with a plan for the next time temptation would come knocking.

I remember the first time someone close to me became disgruntled and refused to repent, I was shocked and deeply hurt. Through our times in the Word, sharing our hearts vulnerably, eating and laughing together I had felt very unified and close. Suddenly, what seemed like overnight, things changed. No longer was she willing and obedient to God, but rather resistant and rebellious. She disconnected and disappeared. I cried, wondering if there was anything I could have done to help her. Somehow I felt responsible.

It was registering to me more and more why the great men and women of the Bible craved consistent time with God. They saw their need to constantly bring their focus back to Him. His omnipotence, omniscience and omnipresence builds our faith to continue to fight the good fight. To overcome and grow. Unlike in the world where our worth is based on our resume, bank account or good looks, as God's children, we get our value from knowing and belonging to God. This prevents those with accolades from becoming prideful and self-righteous as well as those that are less talented from being timid and self-piteous. I saw my need to mature in Christ. I wanted to imitate Paul's desire to know Jesus, Joseph's ability to flee from sin, Daniel's commitment to praying regularly on his knees and David's yearning for time to spend with his God.

Psalm 42:1-2 NIV
As the deer pants for streams of water, so my soul pants for you, my God. [2] My soul thirsts
for God, for the living God. When can I go and meet with God?

I always need the nourishment that God gives. This strengthening of my faith happens when I prioritize time and attention to meeting with Him. Opening my mind and my heart to receive His nutrition builds me up to be an encouragement to those around me. Satan and his demonic forces are always vying for our souls since their only revenge against God is to lure us back into the darkness. With schemes to divide, discourage, deceive and demolish our love and trust for God, ourselves and others.

In my opinion the most successful plot is to distract us from consistently nurturing our relationships with God as our first priority. A chain response to this negligence is that we do not do the mind renewal necessary to view ourselves as God does and so we are riddled with toxic negative self talk. We then become increasingly people focused. Before we know it, we can all be practicing "Churchianity" instead of Christianity. Sadly, I have been guilty here. Falling into the trap of caring too much about people's opinion of me.

Reflection:

Q: Are you practicing Christianity or "Churchianity" today? If the latter, what will you do to change your focus?

Being and staying in awe of God and subsequently growing in our personal holiness does not happen on its own. Rather it is developed when we do what it takes to stay aware of how omnipotent, omniscient and omnipresent God is at all times! God is Holy and so we must be holy. We must set ourselves apart from what the world focuses on. One of the main distractions today can be overuse and content of what we view on the screens.

Q: When you wake up, do you acknowledge God before you reach for your cell phone? If so, why?

Q: Remember David's heart as he yearned to meet with God in Psalm 42:1. Will you choose to imitate this man who revered and honored God?

OMNIPOTENT = ALL POWERFUL:

In the very first chapter of the Bible, God showed his omnipotence by breathing everything seen and unseen into existence. This power is unfathomable to us as humans and is all the more reason for us to stand in "awe" of what God allows us to know about Himself in the Bible!

Genesis 1:1 NKJV
In the beginning God created the heavens and the earth.

Therefore, God is OMNIPOTENT = ALL POWERFUL - yes, He is more powerful than anyone or anything!

OMNISCIENT = ALL KNOWING:

Isaiah teaches us that God knows everything all the time! What an incredible privilege to have Him as our Father who loves us so very much!

Isaiah 40:28 TPT
Don't you know? Haven't you been listening? YAHWEH is the one and only everlasting God, the Creator of all you can see and imagine! He never gets weary or worn out. His intelligence is unlimited; he is never puzzled over what to do!

Thus, God created classical science (what we see) and quantum physics (what we do not see - that which is beyond space and time). Do not be duped that science and God do not mix, rather, since science is simply knowledge, and He is all knowing. Therefore, God is the author of both science and the Bible. In fact, the more you know about something (the science behind anything), the more in awe of our God you should be!

Here we see how God is OMNISCIENT = ALL KNOWING - yes, He knows everything, even our every thought!

OMNIPRESENT = EVERYWHERE ALL THE TIME:

King David shares the truth about God being omnipresent so vividly below:

Psalm 139:7-11 TPT
Where could I go from your Spirit? Where could I run and hide from your face? [8] If I go up to heaven, you're there! If I go down to the realm of the dead, you're there too! [9] If I fly with wings into the shining dawn, you're there! If I fly into the radiant sunset, you're there waiting! [10] Wherever I go, your hand will guide me; your strength will empower me. [11] It's impossible to disappear from you or to ask the darkness to hide me, for your presence is everywhere, bringing light into my night.

"God's omnipotence is like a vast ocean, and we are but tiny drops in its vastness." - Unknown

We see that our God is OMNIPRESENT = EVERYWHERE ALL THE TIME - yes, He is absolutely everywhere at every moment, whereas we cannot even be in two places simultaneously!

When I keep this accurate view of my Lord in the forefront of my thinking then I can more readily adopt the faith to believe that God is always capable! I am safe, I am secure, I am loved, I am enough, and I am worthy since God and His awesomeness reside in me. I get to access this power to mature as His child and be the love force God custom designed for me.

Angel (Holy Spirit) versus Demon (Flesh) Metaphor

Spending time, like you are now, nourishing your faith through the Word, is a big part of how we feed the Holy Spirit in us to have Him dominate the messages sent to our soul (mind and heart). So, the presence of the truth gains the greatest influence over our decisions as they override the sinful urges coming in through our flesh (our five senses).

Do you remember the visual from the chapter on Nourishing the Holy Spirit?

Reflection:

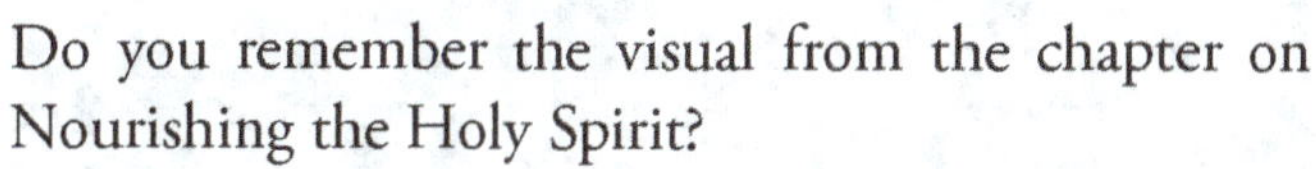

**"God's power is infinite, and his wisdom is unfathomable."
- Albert Einstein**

Q: Are you as aware of this battle as you need to be? If so, do you deliberately direct your attention back to who God is and what pleases Him?

Einstein was right in stating that God's power is infinite and his wisdom unfathomable, however, if we don't spend time meditating on this and continuing to build these memories into our brains then the world will again become our home. Our flesh will take back residence as the head of our household.

Revelation 19:6 NKJV
And I heard, as it were, the voice of a great multitude, as the sound of many waters and as the sound of mighty thunderings, saying, "Alleluia! For the Lord God Omnipotent reigns!

We see here that at the end of time, praises towards our Lord God Omnipotent. We know too that every knee will bow and every tongue will confess that Jesus Christ is Lord (Phil 2:10-11). Focusing on God's power, empowers! Make no mistake, even though we are faithful Disciples today, none of us are beyond being deceived by the spiritual forces of evil in this dark world.

Ephesians 6:10-12 NIV
Finally, be strong in the Lord and in his mighty power. [11] Put on the full armor of God, so that you can take your stand against the devil's schemes. [12] For our struggle is not against flesh and blood, but against the rulers, against the authorities, against the powers of this dark world and against the spiritual forces of evil in the heavenly realms.

OUR BATTLE IS NOT AGAINST FLESH AND BLOOD

Here Paul describes our responsibility to "put on the full armor of God". This does not happen unless we make it happen. Over the years I have been distracted at times by not spending enough time quality washing my mind with the Word. I have been guilty of focusing on people and comparing myself only to despair. I have allowed myself to be riddled with fear over other people's choices. What a waste of time and energy. A huge part of that spiritual armor we are to wear is remembering God and who He is in real time. This is also why the greatest commandment is all about loving God first and wholeheartedly.

Our battle is not against flesh and blood

Mark 12:29-30 NIV
"The most important one," answered Jesus, "is this: 'Hear, O Israel: The Lord our God, the Lord is one. [30] Love the Lord your God with all your heart and with all your soul and with all your mind and with all your strength.'

It all comes back down to our choice to stay focused on the truth, the whole truth and nothing but the truth. So help us God!

Reflection:

Q: What does GOD OMNIPOTENT (all powerful), OMNISCIENT (all knowing) AND OMNIPRESENT (always everywhere) mean to you today?

GOD IS SOVEREIGN:

"God is the ruler with absolute power. He made all things; He is not the work of man's hands, nor a god of man's imaginations." We find the phrase "Sovereign Lord, who made the heavens and the earth and the sea and everything in them," throughout the Scriptures.

> *Jeremiah 32:17 NLT*
> *"O Sovereign LORD! You made the heavens and earth by your strong hand and powerful*
> *arm. Nothing is too hard for you!*

Jeremiah understood who God was and kept his perspective strong by reinforcing the facts. He appreciated God as His Sovereign Lord.

Sovereign meaning ruler, king, and Lord. Scripture often refers to God as the one who rules over all. His most common proper name, Yahweh (see Ex 3:14) is regularly translated as Lord in the English Bible. Lord is found there over 7,000 times as a name of God and specifically as a name of Jesus Christ.

Reflection:

Q: What does God being "Sovereign" in your life mean to you?

DAVID, A MAN IN AWE OF GOD:

There are many wonderful examples in the Bible of men and women who understood revering and honoring God accordingly. King David, who was known as "a man after God's own heart", shares his thoughts in so many of the Psalms giving us a glimpse of his mindset and emotions toward His God.

Psalm 63:1-11 NIV
You, God, are my God, earnestly I seek you; I thirst for you, my whole being longs for you, in a dry and parched land where there is no water. [2] I have seen you in the sanctuary and beheld your power and your glory. [3] Because your love is better than life, my lips will glorify you. [4] I will praise you as long as I live, and in your name I will lift up my hands. [5] I will be fully satisfied as with the richest of foods; with singing lips my mouth will praise you. [6] On my bed I remember you; I think of you through the watches of the night. [7] Because you are my help, I sing in the shadow of your wings. [8] I cling to you; your right hand upholds me. [9] Those who want to kill me will be destroyed; they will go down to the depths of the earth. [10] They will be given over to the sword and become food for jackals. [11] But the king will rejoice in God; all who swear by God will glory in him, while the mouths of liars will be silenced.

This is the focus we want to work towards cultivating everyday!

Reflection:

Q: Are you earnestly focusing on God today? Is your conviction that God's love is better than life?

Since God is omniscient, He knows everything!

Hebrews 4:13 NIV
Nothing in all creation is hidden from God's sight. Everything is uncovered and laid bare before the eyes of him to whom we must give account.

Reflection:

Q: How does the fact that God knows everything about you, including your deepest darkest thoughts, make you feel?

A Christ focused mind and heart

Since God is omnipresent, He is always everywhere!

Jeremiah 23:23-24 NLT
Am I a God who is only close at hand?" says the LORD. "No, I am far away at the same time. [24] Can anyone hide from me in a secret place? Am I not everywhere in all the heavens and earth?" says the LORD.

Proverbs 15:3 NIV
The eyes of the LORD are everywhere, keeping watch on the wicked and the good.

Reflection:

Q: How does God being everywhere all the time make you feel about His ability to be present in your life personally?

To further increase our faith in our incredible God, here are 10 facts about nature and the human body that He created:

Stand in awe!

1. The universe is estimated to be around 13.8 billion years old.
2. There are more stars in the universe than grains of sand on all the beaches on Earth.
3. The intricate and delicate structures of snowflakes are unique, with no two snowflakes being exactly alike!
4. The Grand Canyon, carved by the Colorado River over millions of years, is a testament to the power of erosion.
5. The tallest trees on Earth, known as coast redwoods, can reach heights of over 350 feet (107 meters) and can live for thousands of years.
6. The human brain is the most complex organ in the body, containing around 86 billion neurons.
7. The human eye can distinguish about 10 million different colors.
8. The human nose can remember up to 50,000 different scents.
9. The human heart beats around 100,000 times a day, pumping about 2,000 gallons of blood.
10. The human skin is the largest organ covering an area of about 20 square feet.

It is mind blowing when we stop and ponder on all God is and what He has done, is doing and will do! Since whatever we focus on expands, why not focus on how awesome our God is all the time? God calls us to remember who He is and praise Him for His magnificence because this helps our mindset to be faithful to Him, our God omnipotent, omniscient and omnipresent.

Reflection:

Q: How does this make you feel about the God you serve now?

10 PRACTICALS TO KEEP GOD OMNIPOTENT, OMNISCIENT AND OMNIPRESENT:

1.   Make communicating with God all day in various forms your main goal. Adjusting my paradigm from "having a quiet time", to "walking with my God all day long" has been a game changer in my relationship with Him.

2.   That being said, do make and guard special time set aside every day to have your date with God. Consistency is the best way to breed intimacy. Do not be religious, God cares about your heart. As I've gone through various phases in my life, this has looked different. When I was single, I had all kinds of flexibility to spend ample quality time with God. When I had babies, I would make my time happen during breast-feeding and when they napped. I used my audio Bible when the lights were too dim to read. When our children were toddlers, Chris and I would take turns to be with them so that we could have quality calm time with God individually. Some people can wake up early and be alert and focused, others like to spend time with God later at night. Don't feel guilty if the latter is how you operate best.

Once again it is not about when you spend quality time, it is about setting your heart and mind on God all the time. What has been incredible for me is to get on my knees when I wake up and set up my all day communion with God by making Him my first connection of the day. There is no wrong time to spend with God. Pray for wisdom and make a decision to prioritize time to devote nourishing your love for God.

3.   As well as planning when to have this quality time, what to study (at least a rough idea) is helpful too. This way you don't waste the time you've set aside. I remember my favorite Math teacher saying, "If you fail to plan you plan to fail". The best advice I've been given is to read the whole Bible annually. I love this! Every year I pick out a new version of the Word with a different approach to this plan and that becomes the basis of my time with God every day. I enjoy marking up my Bible as I dig into what's being said. I've had this approach for over 20 years now. I am still amazed by

God's precious Word

numerous new and faith building insights. Many days I veer off into whatever else I may want to study too. Be creative! Use different study guides and concordances. Read spiritual books to help you with your perspective on various passages. Be careful not to rely entirely on these books for your inspiration on what the scripture is saying. I was guilty of this as a younger disciple and am so grateful for the wisdom of one of my mentors as she pointed this out. I have come to a great balance in finding my own insights as well as appreciating those of others. Now I am writing this workbook praying that it can help relate to and inspire you too. Enjoy this incredible journey as you dig deep into God's Word.

4. Include singing to God, even if you don't sing very well. I still sing some worship songs that I learned in my childhood. I think about the words and I offer them as an act of worship to my best friend and my Lord. Some of my favorites are Majesty, As the Deer Pants, Oh Lord I need a mountain to climb on and Amazing Grace. Write your own songs and poems just like David wrote the Psalms. These are also great to sing or pray through. Play your instruments and dance before your Lord. Have a blast as you relish in His presence.

5. Memorize anchor passages from the Word that you ruminate on throughout your day. Over the years I have many incredible scriptures stored in my heart that I am able to bring to mind instantly because I have spent lots of time running them through my mind. When I am faced with adversity, I'm able to access these powerful promises in real time to help me stabilize my thoughts and feelings. Mental and emotional resilience does not happen organically or by default. Be intentional about what you allow your mind to hold onto. I like to refer to this as the Love Zone. This is where God expects us to hang out most of the time (Phil 4:8, 1 Cor 13:1-13, Gal 5:22-25).

6. Develop a practice of Biblical meditation. This has changed and deepened my relationship with God tremendously. Every morning, I meditate for about 20-30 minutes. I include stretching and intentional breathing in my meditation. Access the morning sunlight while doing so. Feeling the sun on my face also helps me to connect with God. God created nature to nurture our souls. Spend time looking up at the sky, appreciating the trees, the clouds, the birds, the breeze and the beauty of nature around you. For more details see Part 2, chapter 17 of this workbook series - Use the Power of Breath and Meditation

7. Confess your sin regularly to God in detail. He loves you and knows your every thought. Confessing helps you to trust God more.

8. Go often to your solitary place to pray. My favorite place is going on prayer walks, especially at night.

9. Be intentionally grateful to God as often as possible. Express your gratitude verbally so that you hear yourself being thankful. Make a decision not to grumble and complain, I remember when we lived in Arizona. When the summer began I told God that I would not grumble about the heat. I did my best not to and I really enjoyed our years in beautiful Phoenix. This helped me guard my heart even during the weeks that averaged a high temperature of 117 degrees.

10. Journal your thoughts and feelings to God often. When I take the time to write down what I am thinking, I see things more clearly and can more readily elaborate on my emotions. This is a great tool to dig deeper into what is underneath my surface emotions.

For further study see Psalm 91, all about God our protector. When we are fearful we cannot be faithful. Also see Prov 18:10; Ps 147:6,10-11; 146:6-9; 145:8, 16-21; 142:1-7;

Adopt the above practicals and others you may like, one at a time. Be gracious and patient with yourself, accept God's love and forgiveness and choose to love and forgive yourself. It is not a contest. God loves you the most whether you are spending consistent times with Him or whether you are struggling to do so. His love for us NEVER CHANGES. We change for the worst if we are not deliberate and intentional about growing spiritually.

In Summary:

This is your personal walk with God that you are investing in. God loves you completely as is, He also expects you to grow. God is the ultimate superpower and we get to tap into His strength by remembering His Omnipotence, Omniscience and Omnipresence. When you love Him first you will be equipped to love others as you love yourself.

Chapter 6

LOVE THE LORD: EMBRACING TRANSFORMING MERCY AND AMAZING GRACE

Though God has over 100 different names describing Himself throughout the Scriptures, His attributes are rooted in two primary dimensions. The first being His grace and mercy while the second is God's justice and judgment. Having a healthy balanced perspective is essential to maturing in our relationship with God.

Fire and Brimstone

That way we do not abuse His kindness nor wallow in His discipline.

As I previously shared, growing up I paid more attention to God being my judge than realizing He was gracious too. I feared the fiery brimstone that awaited me if I wasn't good enough. If you were raised in somewhat of a religious environment perhaps you too lean more one way or the other. Mercy and grace are not a "get out of jail free card", neither is His judgment unjust.

As a disciple, when I sinned, my tendency was to be very hard on myself. I was angry for messing up and felt like I deserved to be punished. Figuratively I pulled out the whip in condemnation of self. I felt like God was mad at me and that I had to earn His grace back by being as perfect as possible, all the time. Since I was not strong in mercy and grace, I also wrestled to extend these beautiful qualities. Especially to those closest to me, my wonderful husband, awesome children and others that I loved dearly. This distorted view of mercy and judgement left me feeling guilty, even after I had repented. My burden was heavy and my yoke felt difficult.

That heavy burdened truck was how I felt sometimes!

Thankfully, heavy burdens were never Jesus' plan for us. The problem is never on God's part or with His design. The issue was my lack of understanding and embracing His transforming mercy and His amazing grace.

Matthew 11:28-30 NIV
"Come to me, all you who are weary and burdened, and I will give you rest. [29] Take my yoke upon you and learn from me, for I am gentle and humble in heart, and you will find rest for your souls. [30] For my yoke is easy and my burden is light."

If we remain in a distorted state of understanding who God really is, this immaturity will in time be our demise. We will lose heart and give up. As I prayed, confessed and studied the Word, I began to learn to grasp mercy and grace as God intended. I began to understand that without embracing and passing on both of these qualities I could not grow up in my salvation as I should. As I mentioned reading Jerry Bridges' two books, "The Practice of Godliness" and "The Pursuit of Holiness", also helped me to clarify where I had to shift my paradigm and what I needed to repent of. My view of grace was not biblically sound. I was self reliant and missing the freedom that God's transforming mercy and amazing grace.

Romans 1:7 NIrV
I am sending this letter to all of you in Rome. You are loved by God and appointed to be his holy people. May God our Father and the Lord Jesus Christ give you grace and peace.

Paul reminds the Roman disciples that in order to be holy we must receive the grace God gives us. As we do, His peace will prevail replacing any false guilt, inadequacy or unworthiness. Thanks to His transforming mercy and amazing grace, we are enough and complete!

Colossians 2:9-10 NLT
For in Christ lives all the fullness of God in a human body. [10] So you also are complete through your union with Christ, who is the head over every ruler and authority.

Perhaps I am not alone in this misconception? Ignorant of the real power of mercy and grace, their deep significance and the importance of being rooted and confident in them. We must train them to become our default mindset that fuel our love for God, ourselves and others.

Strong in Mercy and Grace

Hebrews 4:16 NIV
Let us then approach God's throne of grace with confidence, so that we may receive mercy and find grace to help us in our time of need.

Learning that we continue to need mercy and grace in order to tap into the power God provides, is incredible. Seeing that God's throne is one of grace and that I am to approach God with confidence thanks to His grace, humbles and empowers me.

Reflection:

Q: What do mercy and grace mean to you right now?

Q: What is the difference to you between mercy and grace?

The definitions of mercy and grace:
The word "mercy" comes from the Medieval Latin word "merced" or "mercies", which means "price paid". It has the connotation of forgiveness, benevolence and kindness.

God's "grace" is usually defined as undeserved favor. Grace cannot be earned, rather it is something that is freely given. We count on God's grace as the bridge he built in our relationship with him.

Thank You

What is the difference between mercy and grace in the Bible? The simplest way to understand the difference between grace and mercy is that they are flip sides of the coin of God's love. His mercy is NOT giving us what we DO DESERVE. And God's grace is GIVING us what we DO NOT DESERVE.

This is absolutely incredible since we do deserve death (Rom 6:23) and we do not deserve forgiveness and the promise of his Holy Spirit (Acts 2:38) along with a full beautiful life in His Kingdom. If this was all we got as disciples, should it not be sufficient?

Reflection:

Q: How grateful are you today for God's mercy and grace? Why?

What mercy is not:
We see a vivid example of lack of mercy when the Egyptians forced the Israelites into slavery. Then when Moses came to set them free, rather than let them go, they were treated with even less mercy.

> *Exodus 1:13-14 NLT*
> *So the Egyptians worked the people of Israel without mercy. [14] They made their lives bitter, forcing them to mix mortar and make bricks and do all the work in the fields. They were ruthless in all their demands.*

This is what our lives are like spiritually speaking without embracing and generously extending mercy and grace.

A closer look at Mercy:
From the beginning God demonstrates His mercy in a powerful way. We see how he showered it towards Lot when he deserved to die in Gomorrah. We see God's hand of mercy on Joseph who was sold by his own brothers as a slave and yet rose to become second to Pharaoh in Egypt. By God's mercy the Israelites were spared from a terrible famine. Moses understood that sin requires mercy and so he asked God to be merciful when the people rebelled (Num 11:11).

"You shall not make for yourself a carved image-any likeness of anything that is in heaven above, or that is in the earth beneath, or that is in the water under the earth; [5] you shall not bow down to them nor serve them. For I, the LORD your God, am a jealous God, visiting the iniquity of the fathers upon the children to the third and fourth generations of those who hate Me, [6] but showing mercy to thousands, to those who love Me and keep My commandments. Exodus 20:4-6 NKJV

Within minutes or hours of spending quality time with God it is possible for my mind to drift towards the lure of false gods. I can get critical of my amazing husband, fearful for my children and faithless about choices being made around me in the government or the church. I have become weary at times of reaching out to so many that seem only to reject Jesus. I have also experienced being heavily burdened when I've failed to surrender other's pain at the Cross instead of trying to fix things myself.

This is why I need to "write His Words in my mind and on my heart" (memorize and meditate) and do my best to bring them to my attention in the moment in order to counteract the seductive force of fear, bitterness, self righteousness or weariness that come knocking.

Proverbs 7:1-3 NIrV
My son, obey my words. Store up my commands inside you. [2] Obey my commands and you will live. Guard my teachings as you would guard your own eyes. [3] Tie them on your fingers. Write them on the tablet of your heart.

The longer I stay faithful as a disciple of Jesus, the more I realize I need mercy and grace on my best day. As I grow in my love and appreciation for my Savior I am more sensitized to my wicked thoughts, uncontrolled tongue and deceitful heart. This makes me so grateful that I have the privilege to continue to choose to accept the redeeming power of God's love expressed in his mercy and grace.
Interestingly in the Old Testament, the Ark of the Covenant which was the sacred container housing the Ten Commandments had a seat called the Mercy Seat. This was a significant piece of furniture described in the books of Exodus and Leviticus. The Mercy Seat was a solid gold lid that covered the Ark and had

two cherubim (angelic figures) on either end, with their wings outstretched above it. In the context of Jewish worship, the Mercy Seat symbolized the presence of God and was the place where God would meet with His people. It was on this seat that the High Priest would sprinkle the blood of the sacrificial animals during the Day of Atonement (Yom Kippur) as a means of atoning for the sins of the people. This act represented God's willingness to forgive and show mercy to His people, highlighting the themes of forgiveness and compassion in the Old Testament. The Mercy Seat served as a powerful symbol of God's mercy and the possibility of reconciliation between God and humanity.

In the New Testament, Jesus' death on the Cross is our Mercy Seat, his blood shed is our forgiveness. This is where He did not give us the death we do deserve since he paid the price on our behalf.

Ephesians 1:7 NIrV
We have been set free because of what Christ has done. Because he bled and died our
sins have been forgiven. We have been set free because God's grace is so rich.

David is such a great example of a man knowing he desperately needed God's mercy. He could trust it. He was aware that goodness and mercy would follow him all the days of his life.

Psalm 6:2 NIrV
LORD, have mercy on me. I'm so weak. LORD, heal me. My body is full of pain.

Reflection:

Q: Do you understand that you are weak and need mercy on your best day? If so, do you ask God to have mercy on you often?

David understood that mercy and love went hand in hand and that both are founded in truth. Since mercy builds us up, David rejoiced in it since he was saved from trouble time and time again (Ps 31:7-9). We also see how David models showing mercy to King Saul who was venomously out to kill him.

1 Samuel 24:10 NLT
This very day you can see with your own eyes it isn't true. For the LORD placed you at my
mercy back there in the cave. Some of my men told me to kill you, but I spared you. For I
said, 'I will never harm the king-he is the LORD's anointed one.'

Reflection:

Q: What would you have done in David's shoes?

Q: Who have you shown mercy to recently?

Hosea 6:6 states, "For I desire mercy, not sacrifice, and acknowledgment of God rather than burnt offerings."

This verse emphasizes God's desire for genuine compassion and a relationship with us over mere ritualistic compliance. It highlights the importance of internal devotion and ethical behavior rather than external religious practices. God values a heart that seeks to know Him and to show mercy to others, indicating that true worship flows from a place of love and understanding rather than mere observance of traditions.

Reflection:

Q: Is it easy for you to "play church" without going to God with your sin and seeking his mercy?

Q:What does this look like for you?

One of my favorite memory scriptures is:

Micah 6:8 NLT
No, O people, the LORD has told you what is good, and this is what he requires of you: to do what is right, to love mercy, and to walk humbly with your God.

Love Mercy

Not only is showing mercy vital, we must love to show mercy to others. This is a challenge for me sometimes. I feel like after a certain amount of mercy given, I can run out of it, getting bitter and self righteous. I am continuing to learn to set healthy boundaries, while being conscious not to withhold being merciful. "Who am I?" This is a good reframing question for me to come back to my senses. When I remember that I desperately need mercy everyday.

In the New Testament Paul taps into the power of God's mercy to fuel our passion to share the Good News with all who are willing to listen.

> *2 Corinthians 3:18 - 4:2 NIrV*
> *None of our faces are covered with a veil. All of us can see the Lord's glory and think deeply about it. So we are being changed to become more like him so that we have more and more glory. And this glory comes from the Lord, who is the Holy Spirit. So because of God's mercy, we have work to do. He has given it to us. And we don't give up. [2] Instead, we have given up doing secret and shameful things. We don't twist God's word. In fact, we do just the opposite. We present the truth plainly. In the sight of God, we make our appeal to everyone's sense of what is right and wrong.*

It's so wonderful to see how embedded mercy needs to be in the mind and heart of all Disciples. We see that many of the Epistles begin and end with an emphasis on grace, mercy and peace. God knows we need to be reminded of the truth concerning His mercy and grace in our lives! To me this is like the biggest hug and token of approval from God himself, telling us repeatedly how sufficient, worthy and all around enough we are to Him.

> *2 John 1:3 NIrV*
> *God the Father and Jesus Christ his Son will give you grace, mercy and peace. These blessings will be with us because we love the truth.*

HIS Mercy is new everyday

A closer look at Grace:

God's grace is showered onto Noah in the very beginning of the Old Testament. Without God giving Noah and his family a way out of the wickedness of the world, they too may eventually have succumbed to it. His grace provided the plan for the ark and the flood.

> **"Grace is not just a little prayer you say before receiving a meal. It is a way to live." - Jackie Windspear**

Genesis 6:8 NKJV
But Noah found grace in the eyes of the LORD.

In the Psalm below, we see a profound confidence in God's grace.

Psalm 84:11 NKJV
For the LORD God is a sun and shield; The LORD will give grace and glory; No good thing will He withhold From those who walk uprightly.

We learn that grace and truth go hand in hand (John 1:14). We see in the book of Acts how grace is at work as many are saved and grow to become vessels of God's love to others (Acts 6:8, 11:23,13:34, 14:26). In Romans we are taught to stand in grace (Rom 5:2, 21) and that grace leads to freedom (Rom 6:14). Paul teaches us that we are who we are, thanks to grace (1 Cor 15:10). We are to depend on God's grace not worldly wisdom (2 Cor 1:12). Grace leads to action and we continue to need grace (2 Cor 6:1, 1 Tim 1:14). Below is my personal favorite fact about grace. This truth has become and remained one of the key meditations of my heart that have altered my paradigm.

Grace is always grateful for the cross

2 Corinthians 12:9 NLT
Each time he said, "My grace is all you need. My power works best in weakness." So now I am glad to boast about my weaknesses, so that the power of Christ can work through me.

Reflection:

Q: Is God's Grace all you need? If so why, if not why not?

Be strong in the grace:

We are to be strong in God's grace, our gratitude for His grace should teach us to say "No" to godlessness. This is so deep-seeded because of the connection between grace and the Cross of Jesus. Our acceptance of His grace shows God that we need, respect and appreciate the sacrifice Jesus made for us when he paid the price for us.

Titus 2:11-12 NIV
For the grace of God has appeared that offers salvation to all people. [12] It teaches us to say "No" to ungodliness and worldly passions, and to live self controlled, upright and godly lives in this present age,

Grace helps us to continue to remember our why. Jesus is our why, he is the way, the truth and the life and thanks to his blood shed, we get to live in grace!

Reflection:

Q: Is grace just a little prayer you say before your meal?

Q: Will you make it your new mindset if you haven't already?

Q: Do you struggle to accept God's grace and mercy for yourself? Hint: if you are prone to condemn yourself then your answer is "Yes".

Can we lose mercy and grace?

The answer is yes we can. Once saved and once mature does not equate to always saved or always mature. Since we need mercy and grace to be saved and we can lose our salvation, we too can lose the gift of God's mercy and grace.

We see that the devil entered Judas Iscariot (one of the 12 Apostles), who proceeded to hang himself shortly thereafter (Luke 22:3). This falling away from grace was because of his choice to deliberately continue to sin. What a sad example of failing to be motivated by grace, even when Jesus was with him in person. None of us are above having mercy and grace leave us too if we return to patterns of deliberate sinful choices.

Hebrews 10:26-31 NIV
If we deliberately keep on sinning after we have received the knowledge of the truth, no sacrifice for sins is left, [27] but only a fearful expectation of judgment and of raging fire that will consume the enemies of God. [28] Anyone who rejected the law of Moses died without mercy on the testimony of two or three witnesses. [29] How much more severely do you think someone deserves to be punished who has trampled the Son of God underfoot, who has treated as an unholy thing the blood of the covenant that sanctified them, and who has insulted the Spirit of grace? [30] For we know him who said, "It is mine to avenge; I will repay," and again, "The Lord will judge his people." [31] It is a dreadful thing to fall into the hands of the living God.

We also see that God took his mercy away from Saul who refused to repent.

2 Samuel 7:15 NKJV
But My mercy shall not depart from him, as I took it from Saul, whom I removed from before you.

Paul addresses the church with the sober fact that grace can be lost too. Grace is activated by our faith and obedience, not because we are good enough to earn it.

Galatians 5:4 NLT
For if you are trying to make yourselves right with God by keeping the law, you have been cut off from Christ! You have fallen away from God's grace.

Both mercy and grace should be deeply woven into the fabric of our daily lives, urging us to embrace the power of these incredible gifts. I am personally so thankful for my wonderful husband who has always demonstrated these precious qualities and in so doing become an inspiration and role model for me. He is brutally honest about his sin and readily accepts, appreciates and extends both mercy and grace without self condemnation.

Romans 8:1-2 NLT
So now there is no condemnation for those who belong to Christ Jesus. [2] And because you belong to him, the power of the life-giving Spirit has freed you from the power of sin that leads to death.

In Summary:

We belong to Christ Jesus and so we are free. In order to stay free we must seize the distinct yet intertwined power of mercy and grace. They are the demonstration of the love of Jesus for us and in turn we gladly share them with others. Grace, far from being a mere prayer, is being given what we do not deserve. Similarly, mercy emerges as a tangible expression of love where God did not give us death, which is clearly what we do deserve. This reflects God's unfailing kindness towards humanity. As we integrate these principles into our lives, we choose not only to be recipients but also conduits of mercy and grace. In this way, we experience the true essence of spiritual maturing, where our hearts are softened, our minds renewed, and our lives become a testament to the transforming mercy and amazing grace that surrounds us.

Power In Grace And Mercy

Chapter 7

LOVE THE LORD: GOD OUR THERAPIST PART A

In recent years there has been a significant increase in the demand for therapy worldwide. Various events have brought about numerous challenges and exposed weaknesses: social fear and isolation, paranoia about illness, addiction to drugs and alcohol, rising anger and impatience, marriage and parenting issues, financial difficulties and uncertainty about the future. Many are riddled with anxiety and depression, succumbing to apathy and laziness. There is also an air of entitlement in some where working hard, full time, is replaced by "get rich quick" fantasies, working the system and taking advantage of government assistance.

Pain is real

Therapy can be very useful. Speaking about our pain is healthy. However, therapy can also be harmful when we believe worldly counsel that contradicts God's Word. It is imperative to continue to armor up spiritually if and when seeking therapy. We must have clear vision, able to discern the disputables from what is sin in order to make Godly decisions.

NEGATIVE EMOTIONS ARE REAL AND COMMON:

Struggling with negative emotions is real and understandable. It is in fact part of normal life. Contrary to what some therapists might suggest, you do not necessarily have a disorder if you are feeling depressed, anxious or angry. The real problem lies with how we process our many thoughts and feelings. At the end of the day we are either managing our minds to be in step with the Spirit or not. So, learning how to regulate our thoughts, God's way, is effective processing of the most turbulent emotions.

For some time, even as a Christian, I condemned myself when I had bouts of fear and anxiety. I would question my connection with God, despite making my best effort at the time to do what was right. It is a sad misnomer to assume that we have sinned when we feel negative emotions. This discouragement simply fuels our already heavy burden. Though feeling anger, sadness, anxiety, fear, resentment, hatred, etc is not in and of itself sin, these will develop into sinful mindsets if we allow ourselves to wallow in them. When we ruminate on negativity we "automatize" it to dominate our thinking.

> *Romans 8:6 NIV*
> *The mind governed by the flesh is death, but the mind governed by the Spirit is life and peace.*

Pessimistic thought patterns often lead to us feeling sorry for ourselves or that we are not good enough. We can become resentful believing that we have been dealt the "short end of the stick". These unregulated thoughts give birth to a dangerous victim mentality. In this state, we do not take responsibility for our choices. We want to blame something or someone for our circumstances and demeanor. We can be easily influenced by unbiblical approaches to solving our issues. Being diagnosed with a disorder or disease can then basically validate the victim in us. This does not happen to all people. For those who really want to change a diagnosis can encourage them in not being alone in their symptoms and the knowledge that they have options. The focus of this chapter is not on psychiatry, labeling or treatment, rather it is about gaining adequate knowledge of these fields along with learning to keep God as our first therapist in order to identify worldly schemes.

Reflection:

Q: How are you responsponding today to whatever turbulence you are wrestling with?

God's plan produces life and peace

The intense negative feelings we all experience are real and valid. However, they do not necessarily equate to us being disordered and in need of medication. Instead they are warning signals that need to be honed in on and unpacked in order to find the root of our anguish. As we actively do the difficult heart work to identify, examine and redirect our thinking into the Love Zone (the way Jesus teaches us to think), in time, our thinking and subsequent feelings change for the better. We are no longer focused on the problem, but the solution. Rather than meditating on the negative such as worry, fear, anger, depression, etc. we are meditating on the truth of Jesus and His power in us. This is not easy and does not happen by osmosis. Rather it takes intentionality and perseverance. It is a skill we need to learn and consistently practice.

Sometimes we feel extremely overwhelmed and it is even hard to believe that we can overcome the insanity we feel inside. This is why we need to realize and embrace the Holy Spirit as our primary source of power and counsel. The intense negative feelings we experience are understandable, valid and definitely need attention. However, they are not the truth of who we are in Christ and they do not reflect the power we have access to when we embrace God's counsel.

1 Corinthians 10:13-15 AMPC
For no temptation (no trial regarded as enticing to sin), [no matter how it comes or where it leads] has overtaken you and laid hold on you that is not common to man [that is, no temptation or trial has come to you that is beyond human resistance and

that is not adjusted and adapted and belonging to human experience, and such as man can bear]. But God is faithful [to His Word and to His compassionate nature], and He [can be trusted] not to let you be tempted and tried and assayed beyond your ability and strength of resistance and power to endure, but with the temptation He will [always] also provide the way out (the means of escape to a landing place), that you may be capable and strong and powerful to bear up under it patiently. [14] Therefore, my dearly beloved, shun (keep clear away from, avoid by flight if need be) any sort of idolatry (of loving or venerating anything more than God). [15] I am speaking as to intelligent (sensible) men. Think over and make up your minds [for yourselves] about what I say. [I appeal to your reason and your discernment in these matters.]

Reflection:

Q: Do you believe that despite how disturbed your emotional state may be, it is not too much for you to gain control over? If so, how? If not, why?

We have the responsibility to take action in changing our thinking. This is discussed in detail in Part 3 of this Workbook Series. We must believe that we can change our thinking and that God will enable us to do so. Changing your mindset is not a one and done. It takes intentionality and consistency. I consider it a privilege to get to do the work of saturating my mind with God's counsel by memorizing scriptures like:

Philippians 4:13 TPT
And I find that the strength of Christ's explosive power infuses me to conquer every difficulty.

Psalm 28:7 NIV
The LORD is my strength and my shield; my heart trusts in him, and he helps me. My heart leaps for joy, and with my song I praise him.

Psalm 23:6 NIV
Surely your goodness and love will follow me all the days of my life, and I will dwell in the house of the LORD forever.

I recall these truths into my mind when I am tempted to listen to counsel other than God's. When I feel so overwhelmed that I want to run away and hide, I acknowledge that my pain is real and valid but not always the truth. Then I do the digging to the bottom of the issue at hand. It is my responsibility to be sober and alert, bringing to my mind and heart God's counsel so as to override the strong influencers around me. By the way, whatever you spend the most time pouring into your mind will become your dominant influence. Adopt God's standards for the quantity and quality of your information influx.

Psalm 19:14 NIV
May these words of my mouth and this meditation of my heart be pleasing in your sight,
LORD, my Rock and my Redeemer.

Reflection:

Q: What is the meditation of your mind and heart most of the time?

BE HUMBLE, SOBER AND ALERT:

People seek out therapy for mind help and being humble to get help is noble. We must remember that the mind is not an organ, rather it is non physical and part of our soul. It is where the spiritual battle is waged, where the processing of all our incoming and upcoming information (through our subconscious mind) happens. In order for our minds to perform optimally, it is imperative to be sober and alert so we can choose to pray, listen to the promptings of the Holy Spirit and make Godly decisions.

1 Peter 4:7 NIV
The end of all things is near. Therefore be alert and of sober mind so that you may pray.

Sober, meaning not under the influence of anything mind altering. Alert is being in a state of watchfulness for possible danger. Being aware in order for us to be in control of where and how we direct our thinking. The danger we all face is being led astray, being duped by the influences of the world around us. This would include the potential of some therapists readily offering quick fixes, some that oppose our standards as Disciples. In the case of someone having marital problems, they may be recommended to end the marriage prematurely. Tragically, there are those suggesting that if you are male and want to be female you have the right to do so. Similarly, being advised to abort a baby because you don't want the responsibility or the burden is unbiblical. Being prescribed mood altering drugs to feel better versus offering a Godly solution on how to actually get well from the inside out, is also not Biblically sound.

I am not a medial professional and am not telling you not to take medicine. I am simply appealing to you to go to God first as your primary therapist and do the work of changing from the inside out regardless of your choice with medication.

As Disciples we must become more skilled in dealing with mind issues. First to be equipped to manage our own minds and then to offer more than just the generic "trust God" to a person who may be really suffering emotionally and mentally. This quest is a journey, not a destination. I am still growing in the disciplines of active listening, appropriate questions to ask, Biblical principles to offer and associated wisdom and practicals that are tried and true. In loving each other we need to receive and give help with how to "trust God".

When we are in pain and seek out mind help we are vulnerable since the expectation should be to be radically open. Transparency is essential in order to give the best perspective on the struggles we face. However, as potentially with professional therapy, we are given direction that veers from God's counsel, we can be lured into adopting the world's methodology versus holding to the Truth.

Reflection:

Q: Are you alert and sober minded wielding the spiritual battle head on? If so, how? If not, why?

SATAN COUNSELED EVE AND SHE TOOK THE BAIT:

Satan successfully played the worldly counsel card with Eve in the garden of Eden. In essence she believed the lies of the serpent instead of standing strong in trusting and obeying God. Satan still uses this very successful scheme today.

> *Genesis 3:1-6 NKJV*
> *Now the serpent was more cunning than any beast of the field which the LORD God*
> *had made. And he said to the woman, "Has God indeed said, 'You shall not eat of every*
> *tree of the garden'?" [2] And the woman said to the serpent, "We may eat the fruit of the*
> *trees of the garden; [3] but of the fruit of the tree which is in the midst of the garden,*
> *God has said, 'You shall not eat it, nor shall you touch it, lest you die.'" [4] Then the*
> *serpent said to the woman, "You will not surely die. [5] For God knows that in the day*
> *you eat of it your eyes will be opened, and you will be like God, knowing good and evil."*
> *[6] So when the woman saw that the tree was good for food, that it was pleasant to the*
> *eyes, and a tree desirable to make one wise, she took of its fruit and ate. She also gave to*
> *her husband with her, and he ate.*

The serpent wanted Eve to disobey God so he had her question God's direction. He proposed a vision of power and freedom, dangling in front of her the idea of feeling even better than she already did. Sadly, despite knowing the truth, she bought into his deceptive words and ate the forbidden fruit. She was so convinced that she persuaded her husband to do the same.

Reflection:

Q: Can you relate to Eve or Adam? If so, how?

It is our responsibility as disciples to uncover and expose deceitful schemes by measuring them with God's Word. We then get to choose to keep God as our standard without compromise. The goal is not just to "feel better" in the moment but actually to "get well" long term from the inside out.

WHAT IS PSYCHIATRY?

Since we are discussing help for the mind, we must talk about psychiatry. The original meaning of the word psychiatry comes from the 19th century, Greek words "psukhē" meaning soul, mind and "iatreia" meaning healing. So psychiatry is supposed to provide "healing for the soul" or "healing for the mind". In principle this is great, however, tragically much of psychiatry today is broken. It has veered so far from actually providing healing. Instead, to many, it is merely a business. In the pursuit of greed, psychiatry is largely married to personal gain and to the pharmaceutical industry (Big Pharma). As a result, oftentimes, therapy includes being labeled with a disorder (disease), followed by a chemical prescription to "heal" your disorder. This way you become an asset since you are forced to come back for your monthly prescription.

Can chemicals heal pain?

Many of the psychotropic medications (mood altering drugs) prescribed dull down the frontal lobe of the human brain and so bring some relief for anxiety, depression, etc. However, they also lower the ability to care as much about relationships and they hinder alertness. Often times the dulling of the drug lessens and this leads to more drugs and/or higher dosages with more side effects.

The "labeled person" can readily adopt a victim mentality in which they do not see changing as their responsibility. This mindset has proven very toxic and is also readily found in people abusing alcohol and other drugs since society has labeled addiction as a disease. The concept of actually denying yourself and "taking the bull by the horns", doing whatever it takes to deal with pain and overcome, sadly can fade into a mere foreign concept.

Reflection:

Q: Do you remember the charge from God's counsel for us to be sober minded and alert? (1 Peter 4:7) Are you obeying this charge?

Q: Are you beginning to see the potential problem? How does this apply personally?

Broken psychiatry is not based on the principles from the scriptures which include confiding in God first, healthy lifestyle, mind renewal and deep connections with like minded people. Placing our hope for "mind healing" into sources that are not directed by the Holy Spirit is reckless and earthly.

> *James 3:13-17 NKJV*
> *Who is wise and understanding among you? Let him show by good conduct that his works are done in the meekness of wisdom. [14] But if you have bitter envy and self-seeking in your hearts, do not boast and lie against the truth. [15] This wisdom does not descend from above, but is earthly, sensual, demonic. [16] For where envy and self-seeking exist, confusion and every evil thing are there. [17] But the wisdom that is from above is first pure, then peaceable, gentle, willing to yield, full of mercy and good fruits, without partiality and without hypocrisy.*

I am not a medical professional and do not claim for anything I say to be assumed as medical advice. I am a faithful disciple of Jesus and simply want to appeal to my spiritual family to make sure that before adopting worldly methodology to guide your mental wellbeing, embrace the power and principles God makes readily available first. True healing for the soul can ultimately only come from God. We may use tools that are disputable when we need extra help, however making and keeping the Holy Spirit as our first and primary therapist should not be compromised.

> **"In truth, the chemical imbalance notion was always a kind of urban legend, never a theory seriously propounded by well-informed psychiatrists." - Ronald Pies, July 11, 2011 in Psychiatric Times**

The majority of people seeking healing for the mind in psychiatry get shuffled in and out of the same offices every month, asked the mandatory questions and then prescribed drugs with negative side effects. Many are told that they have a chemical imbalance or that they have depleted their dopamine.

Did you know that this "chemical imbalance" statement has never been scientifically proven?
The "you have a chemical imbalance" is used as a marketing lie to manipulate ignorant vulnerable people into believing that their only hope for happiness lies in being dependent on a psychiatrist and a pill for the rest of their lives. This, oftentimes, becomes a combination of several pills with sad side effects. A perfect way to guarantee repeat customers.

LOOK AT THE FACTS AND MAKE WISE CHOICES ACCORDINGLY:

For more information about the truth behind psychiatry today see Dr Peter Breggin, an American psychiatrist, who has the unique benefit of being in this field since the introduction of psychiatric medication to the present day. He has a Bird's Eye view on how the approach to mental challenges as well as the effects of these drugs is a dismal sight. He is known for his bold criticism of the pharmaceutical industry and the overprescription of psychiatric medication. He is also an advocate for alternative treatments and therapy. He notes that in the past half a century there has been a drastic rise in general mental mismanagement, obesity and overall well being in humanity on a worldwide level. Some of the books he has written include:

"Toxic Psychiatry: Why Therapy, Empathy and Love Must Replace the Drugs, Electroshock, and Biochemical Theories of the 'New Psychiatry'"
"Psychiatric Drug Withdrawal: A Guide for Prescribers, Therapists, Patients and their Families"
"Medication Madness: A Psychiatrist Exposes the Dangers of Mood-Altering Medications"
"Talking Back to Prozac: What Doctors Won't Tell You About Today's Most Controversial Drug"
"Guilt, Shame, and Anxiety: Understanding and Overcoming Negative Emotions"

Dr. Breggin's work has been influential in raising awareness about the risks and limitations of psychiatric medications.

Reflection:

Q: How do you feel about psychiatry and psychotropic medication today?

GOD IS OUR FIRST AND PRIMARY SOURCE OF THERAPY:

As discussed in Chapter 3, Disciples have unlimited, complementary and readily available 24/7 therapy from God Himself! Through the Holy Spirit and the Word, God guides and advises us all day, everyday. The caveat is whether or not we will be sober minded and alert in order to listen as well as humble enough to obey.

John 14:24, 26 NIV
But the Advocate, the Holy Spirit, whom the Father will send in my name, will teach
you all things and will remind you of everything I have said to you.

Reflection:

Q: Are you seeking counsel first from the Holy Spirit on everything?

Q: What was the most recent issue you wrestled with and asked for guidance on?

Jesus taught His disciples that it was beneficial for Him to leave the earth because then He would send His Holy Spirit to guide and comfort them. He is our counselor and we get to be in close fellowship with Him.

John 16:7 AMPC
However, I am telling you nothing but the truth when I say it is profitable (good, expedient, advantageous) for you that I go away. Because if I do not go away, the Comforter (Counselor, Helper, Advocate, Intercessor, Strengthener, Standby) will not come to you [into close fellowship with you]; but if I go away, I will send Him to you [to be in close fellowship with you].

Reflection:

Q: Are you in close fellowship with the Holy Spirit?

The Holy Spirit is our first therapist

Q: If so, what does this look like for you?

OUR SECOND SOURCE OF THERAPY IS LIKE MINDED DISCIPLING:

As a Christian I have confessed impurity, jealousy, self righteousness, people pleasing, lying, gossip, disrespect, fear, anger and so much more. I continue to need much counsel from my fellow disciples to draw out the deep waters of my heart in order to identify my sin and get in touch with the extent of it. (Prov 20:5)

Embracing and practicing the one another scriptures of the Bible is our second valuable source of therapy.

> *Matthew 26:37-38 NIrV*
> *He took Peter and the two sons of Zebedee along with him. He began to be sad and troubled. [38] Then he said to them, "My soul is very sad. I feel close to death. Stay here. Keep watch with me."*

Just like Jesus asked his disciples to pray with him as he shared his burden with them, so too we are to open our hearts and minds to like minded disciples, giving and receiving counsel from each other.

Disciples love Jesus together

In essence "Discipling" could be referred to as "Prayer Partners" or "Spiritual Accountability Partners", etc and should simply be descriptive of relationships that practice the "one another" and "each other" directives from the Word.

As disciples we choose God as our primary therapist and then we understand the value of seeking advice and counsel from people. In some cases there is also value in seeking out professional input.

Please note that when you seek counsel, you are seeking input or advice. This does not mean that whatever anybody says is going to be the best route of action for you. It is each individual's responsibility as a grown adult to be educated on the matter at hand. Then to seek out much counsel (first from the Holy Spirit and the Word), and then to weigh all the information gleaned in order to make your own decision.

Some have abused discipling relationships by lording over others and making advice seem like "permission".

Scriptures teaching on this issue:

> *Proverbs 11:14 NKJV*
> *Where there is no counsel, the people fall; But in the multitude of counselors there is safety.*

> *Proverbs 12:15 NKJV*
> *The way of a fool is right in his own eyes, But he who heeds counsel is wise.*

> *Proverbs 15:22 NKJV*
> *Without counsel, plans go awry, But in the multitude of counselors they are established.*

> *Proverbs 19:20 NKJV*
> *Listen to counsel and receive instruction, That you may be wise in your latter days.*

I see the Proverbs as shots of wisdom. Wisdom begins with honesty. If we are all honest we will admit that never before have we been in the exact situations that we currently face. Be humble and honest, admit that you need help. Open your heart and mind to the discipline of giving and receiving counsel. Consider prayerfully what is said, measure it with the scriptures and make your own decision taking full responsibility for the outcome.

Reflection:

Q: Do you seek counsel from God first and then others? If not, why?

Q: Do you realize that it is your responsibility to make your own decision as you prayerfully weigh the Word and the other advice? Nobody should be telling you what to do.

"Honesty is the first chapter in the book of wisdom." - Thomas Jefferson

In Summary:

God gives us His Holy Spirit to be our primary guide and counselor. Turn to him as such. Secondly appreciate and glean counsel from trusted sources around you. If and when seeking professional counsel, do so remembering "who" you are and "who's" you are. Do not allow the world to mold you.

Chapter 8

LOVE THE LORD: GOD OUR THERAPIST PART B

In order to have deep convictions that the Holy Spirit is our internal, omnipresent counselor we must know what the Bible teaches about this topic. Below are four "whys" helping us to embrace this truth.

WHY TRUST GOD AS YOUR PRIMARY THERAPIST?

1. God knows every single thing about us:

God does not assume who we are and what is happening in our mind and heart. He created us and carefully knit us together cell by cell. He knows our every thought. David understood this and therefore deeply trusted God.

God my therapist

1 Chronicles 28:9 NIrV
"My son Solomon, always remember
the God of your father. Serve him with all your heart. Do it with a mind that wants to obey him. The LORD looks deep down inside every heart. He understands every desire and every thought. If you look to him, you will find him. But if you desert him, he will turn his back on you forever.

From birth God also gifts each of us with a conscience which is the internal voice letting us know right from wrong. Unfortunately, as we discover deliberate sin, we sear this voice, numbing these warning signals. At baptism, we are given the Holy Spirit, God in us, to guide, counsel and be our advocate. God has done everything to set us up for success. Our job is to manage our minds and choose love and obedience by turning constantly to our first and primary source of therapy, God Himself.

Reflection:

Q: Do you believe that God knows you completely and loves you unconditionally?

Q: Do you trust God with every part of your heart?

2. God keeps it simple:

God gave Adam and Eve paradise with one stipulation. Clear and simple.

> *Genesis 2:16-17 NIV*
> *And the LORD God commanded the man, "You are free to eat from any tree in the garden; [17] but you must not eat from the tree of the knowledge of good and evil, for when you eat from it you will certainly die."*

Today, God continues to simply call us to love and obey Him. The problem is that we allow our minds to deviate from the truth, wandering and ruminating in places that are very dangerous. We see that even the first two humans, Adam and Eve, did not keep their minds set on what God guided and counseled them to do. Instead they chose to listen and obey the counsel of the serpent.

Make no mistake, this remains our battle today. God's love language is obedience (John 14:23-24). Paul makes it so clear when he commissions us to do everything in love. This is "Love Zone" living, which is the only place we thrive. God keeps it simple, let's trust and obey for there truly is no other way to be happy in Jesus.

> *1 Corinthians 16:14 NKJV*
> *Let all that you do be done with love.*

Reflection:

Q: How did Adam and Eve's choice to disobey the counsel of God work out for them?

Q: Are you allowing anyone else's counsel to steer you away from loving God?

Q: If so, who are you listening to and what are you doing?

3. There are terrible consequences to not trusting God:

Shame, fear, pain, blame shifting, banishment and more followed Adam and Eve in their decision to take their focus off God's counsel and to listen to what their itching ears wanted to hear.

> *Genesis 4:7 NLT*
> *At that moment their eyes were opened, and they suddenly felt shame at their nakedness. So they sewed fig leaves together to cover themselves.*

> *Genesis 3:10 NIrV*
> *"I heard you in the garden," the man answered. "I was afraid, because I was naked. So I hid."*

> *Genesis 3:16 and 19 NIrV*
> *The LORD God said to the woman, "I will increase your pain when you give birth. You will be in great pain when you have children. You will long for your husband. And he will rule over you." [19] You will have to work hard and sweat a lot to produce the food you eat. You were made out of the ground. You will return to it when you die. You are dust, and you will return to dust."*

> *Genesis 3:23-24 NIrV*
> *So the LORD God drove the man out of the Garden of Eden. He sent the man to farm the ground he had been made from. [24] The LORD God drove him out and then placed angels on the east side of the garden. He also placed there a flaming sword that flashed back and forth. The angels and the sword guarded the way to the tree of life.*

Reflection:

Q: Was the momentary satisfaction of eating the fruit worth it for Adam and Eve?

At any time they could have taken a deep breath or two and remembered that God's counsel always wins, no matter how appealing anything else sounds. They also could have told the serpent that they needed to seek more counsel from God before making a rash emotional decision.

Reflection:

Q: Do you make rash emotional decisions without remembering God's counsel? If so, how is that working out for you?

4. God provides us with exactly how to handle negative emotions:

In the very beginning of the Bible, we see a perfect example of how God counseled Cain when he was in a pattern of negative thinking.

> *Genesis 4:6-7 NIrV*
> *Then the LORD said to Cain, "Why are you angry? Why are you looking so sad? [7] Do what is right and then you will be accepted. If you don't do what is right, sin is waiting at your door to grab you. It desires to control you. But you must rule over it."*

God approaches Cain with a question to help him think about his thinking and feelings. He's attempting to draw Cain out. Whether it is handling our own emotional battles or helping someone else, the same principle should be followed.

> *Proverbs 20:5 NIrV*
> *The purposes of a person's heart are like deep water. But one who has understanding brings them out.*

God then describes to Cain what He sees on his face and in his demeanor. He asks Cain why he is feeling these things. God knew the answer but He was giving Cain an opportunity to examine his own mind and heart and then verbalize the truth. Unfortunately Cain chooses to shut down and be silent, an obviously bad choice.

When we do not talk about our challenging emotions they remain only in our own head and quickly become "stinking thinking!" Despite his silence God gives him very clear and simple directions as to how to "fix" his problem. The answer is to do what is right, not clam up until you feel like doing what is right. He also lets him know the consequences of ignoring his counsel.

Reflection:

Q: How did Cain respond?

Q: Are you prone to shutting down?

Genesis 4:8 NIrV
Cain said to his brother Abel, "Let's go out to the field." So they went out. There Cain attacked his brother Abel and killed him.

Unconfessed sinful thinking and emotions will lead to destruction. Cain's rebellion made him the first ever murderer. He continued to deny the truth and resist God's counsel and as a result he lived in misery for the rest of his life.

Genesis 4:9-12 NIrV
Then the LORD said to Cain, "Where is your brother Abel?" "I don't know," Cain replied. "Am I supposed to take care of my brother?" [10] The LORD said, "What have you done? Listen! Your brother's blood is crying out to me from the ground. [11] So I am putting a curse on you. I am driving you away from this ground. It has opened its mouth to receive your brother's blood from your hand. [12] When you farm the land, it will not produce its crops for you anymore. You will be a restless person who wanders around on the earth."

Reflection:

Q: Did he regret his lack of love for God for the rest of his life?

Q: Is this really living or simply existing?

Q: Could he have decided to be humble and master his sin at any time?

Q: Is there any sinful pattern that you have not mastered in your life? Is your conscience being bothered at all? If so, what is it?

God is so extremely gracious and as we see with Cain, still gave him mercy, even after his defiant behavior. Let us not take advantage of God's grace, but rather learn to embrace it as an essential element of who He is by appreciating Him as our Master Therapist and ultimate source of counsel.

> **"Insanity is doing the same thing over and over and over again and expecting different results." - attributed to Albert Einstein**

We can change our behavior by changing our thinking and yielding to God's therapy, His plan of treatment. This is a decision. Let us learn from Eve, Adam and Cain by choosing to respect, love and obey God's counsel.

SOME OBSERVATIONS:

It has been painful to see several disciples engaged in psychiatry, on medication and slowly drifting away from God. Recently I was spending time with a dear sister who battles depression and anxiety. She is barely hanging onto her relationship with God. She told me that her connection with God is suffering because of all the medication she's on. Despite the fact that she is aware of this, she still believes that weaning off, even some of it, is too daunting for her. (Always make sure that if you decide to wean off prescription drugs, do so under the supervision of a medical professional).

Another older sister had been on a cocktail of psychotropic drugs for years because she believed the lie that she was chemically imbalanced. Once she learned the truth, she weaned off under medical supervision and has had more clarity and deeper connectivity since.

I remember another disciple who had come from a background of abusing drugs and alcohol. While going through a rough time he was encouraged by his family to turn to psychiatry and medication. After being convinced that he had a chemical imbalance, taking addictive psychotropic medication seemed justified. In time he was put on higher dosages. He continued to dull down and check out by also drinking alcohol again. Shortly afterwards he was fired from his job, isolated in his dependence on substances and disconnected relationally.

I realized how easy it was to start taking mood altering medicine when I was getting my annual check up from my general doctor. She recommended psychotropic drugs to me since she knew of some of the emotional pain I was facing. Something registered inside me to take this suggestion as a wake up call. I needed to learn how to do a much better job of managing my mind and making sure that I was listening first to God's counsel. The below scripture has become an anchor for my mind.

Philippians 4:4-8 NIV
Rejoice in the Lord always. I will say it again: Rejoice! [5] Let your gentleness be evident to all. The Lord is near. [6] Do not be anxious about anything, but in every situation, by prayer and petition, with thanksgiving, present your requests to God. [7] And the peace of God, which transcends all understanding, will guard your hearts and your minds in

> *Christ Jesus. [8] Finally, brothers and sisters, whatever is true, whatever is noble, whatever is right, whatever is pure, whatever is lovely, whatever is admirable—if anything is excellent or praiseworthy—think about such things.*

God says to make Him our joy always. Not our spouses, children, careers, finances or anything else. This was my sin, I had begun to overthink bad decisions being made by those I loved. It takes discipline and intentionality to redirect anxious fearful thinking back into whatever is true, noble, right, pure, lovely, admirable, excellent and praiseworthy. (More specifics on this topic in Part 3 of this Workbook Series).

Without doing the work to be at peace, we are vulnerable to all kinds of toxic influences. It is with this concern that I simply appeal to every Disciple. Do not simply conform to the pattern of modern psychiatry but be transformed by the truth, knowing and keeping the Holy Spirit as our first therapist, our compass for discerning counsel from others. By no means am I saying you do not have the freedom as a disciple to see a professional or take medication. I am saying that you have a responsibility as a follower of Jesus to thoroughly research the truth behind what is being said and the full extent of the side effects of what is being prescribed. With accurate information you are more equipped to make Godly decisions.

Our physical health also greatly impacts our mental wellbeing. The food industry in America, known as the Modern American Diet (M.A.D.) or Big Food, is harming us. We have substituted real food for food-like substances. God created us to eat real food with a peaceful mindset. We should all strive for a real food diet where we eat when we are hungry (not grazing like a cow), and stop when we are satisfied (not stuffed like a turkey).

Reflection:

Q: How often do psychiatrists examine a person's diet and other lifestyle and thinking choices before prescribing drugs?

There are also many natural remedies to improve our mindsets. Things such as: sufficient exercise, getting appropriate sun exposure, breathing intentionally, meditating, adopting new hobbies, making more meaningful connections with actual people, limiting screen time especially scrolling on social media networks, finding our security and purpose in who God is and who He created us to be, quality sleep, cold plunging, heat therapy, caffeine moderation, acupressure, acupuncture and this list is not exhaustive.

Nature Nurtures

Reflection:

Q: How often do psychiatrists prescribe these natural approaches before handing out prescriptions?

In Summary:

Know why and how God counsels you and practice living with these firm convictions. Consider the spiritual impact of what psychiatrists prescribe and others advise. Count the cost thoroughly and make your own decisions. Adopt as a lifestyle as many as possible of the healthy natural remedies readily available to help you manage your mind and your mood.

Chapter 9

LOVE THE LORD: BE A GODLY PARENT

Children are a wonderful reward from God. He gives Parents an incredible amount of power over their children. They are completely vulnerable and helpless, one hundred percent dependent on their caregivers.

Psalm 127:3 NIrV
Children are a gift from the LORD. They are a reward from him.

As a parent myself I am reminded of the famous quote by Spider-Man:

"With great power comes great responsibility" - Ben Parker

God expects us to be responsible for our children by training them to be Godly. He values obedience and honor. God desires parents to obey and honor Him as we train our children to obey and respect us. Then, in time, they will prayerfully learn to obey and honor God too.

Ephesians 6:1-3 NLT
Children, obey your parents because you belong to the Lord, for this is the right thing to do. [2] "Honor your father and mother." This is the first commandment with a promise: [3] If you honor your father and mother, "things will go well for you, and you will have a long life on the earth."

Think about the incredible promises that go along with obedience and honor/respect. Don't you want "things to go well" for your children and for them to have a "long life" on the earth? The answer here is a resounding yes! However, these qualities do not just automatically appear in our children. Have you ever been around a toddler that's new favorite word is, "Mine"?

Spending adequate quality time with them, having fun, teaching them Bible convictions and setting an example of overall wellbeing are all essential in order to be Godly parents. If we do not train our children, make no mistake the world will. Everyday they are inundated with an influx of information and worldly wisdom from their instructors, peers and social media. Do not be deceived and naive about how wicked the world is and what our children hear and see at school and online. I remember our Son, at only 5 years old, coming home from preschool on the bus and asking me about the meaning of a certain profane word.

Spending quality time is necessary

120

Deuteronomy 6:4-7 NIrV
Israel, listen to me. The LORD is our God. The LORD is the one and only God. [5]
Love the LORD your God with all your heart and with all your soul. Love him with all
your strength. [6] The commandments I give you today must be in your hearts. [7] Make
sure your children learn them. Talk about them when you are at home. Talk about them
when you walk along the road. Speak about them when you go to bed. And speak about
them when you get up.

Reflection:

Q: Parents, are you as eager to train your children to be Godly as you were to have them? If so, how are you doing so practically? If not, will you make Godly training a priority?

DISCIPLINE - AN ESSENTIAL AND GODLY PRACTICE:

God says we are all disciplined and that He does so for our good. I am so grateful for my amazing parents who took the time and energy necessary to do the best they could to teach and discipline us. I remember being much more regulated in my decision making since I knew there would be a painful consequence if I just did what I felt like rather than what was right. One night I disobeyed curfew and thought I could just sneak into the house without anyone knowing. I will never forget the look of disappointment on my wonderful Father's face as he sat in the dark waiting for me to come home. Dad and Mom, I am sorry again for the stress I caused both of you. It is indeed true that once you have children of your own, you begin to understand the anguish that parents endure when faced with disobedient and disrespectful children.

However, what I have come to embrace is that since God always works for my good (Rom 8:28), my children are my personal spiritual trainers. It is thanks to them that I am much more God reliant. I can recall several times in my life when God allowed pain to get my attention. This was His love and discipline calling me to repent and mature.

Revelation 3:19 NIV
Those whom I love I rebuke and discipline. So be earnest and repent.

The charge to train our children includes disciplining them. If we fail to practice discipline there will be a time when we "love" our children but we do not "like" them. Along with disciplining them we must be sure to forgive them every day as we also humbly ask for forgiveness from them when we sin. Otherwise Parents can and do actually become very embittered towards their children and vice versa.

The issue of discipline has become so controversial. On the one hand it is totally understandable since sadly, many think that disciplining a child is a license to abuse them. Many people are so bent up with their own sin and it is the overflow of this turmoil that spills onto their children. This is very real and so tragic. Of course abuse in whatever form, towards anyone, anytime is sin and does not please God.

Ephesians 6:4 NLT
Fathers, do not provoke your children to anger by the way you treat them. Rather, bring
them up with the discipline and instruction that comes from the Lord.

HOW TO PRACTICE GODLY DISCIPLINE:

There is a Godly approach to discipline that yields incredible peace. Godly discipline is practiced with all the qualities of love described in the scriptures below:

1 Corinthians 13:4-8a NIrV
Love is patient. Love is kind. It does not want what belongs to others. It does not brag. It is
not proud. [5] It does not dishonor other people. It does not look out for its own interests.
It does not easily become angry. It does not keep track of other people's wrongs. [6] Love is
not happy with evil. But it is full of joy when the truth is spoken. [7] It always protects. It
always trusts. It always hopes. It never gives up. [8] Love never fails.

Galatians 5:22-23 NIrV
But the fruit the Holy Spirit produces is love, joy and peace. It is being patient, kind and
good. It is being faithful [23] and gentle and having control of oneself. There is no law
against things of that kind.

It is patient and kind because you as a Godly parent are consistently instructing and training your children in respect and obedience. You are meeting them at their level and making sure they understand the difference between making a mistake versus willfully making a bad choice. They know that their choice was bad and that they are not bad. You never discipline for a mistake. They also understand what the consequences will be for deliberate disobedience and disrespect. You never ever discipline your child out of sinful anger. We can be indignant about their bad choices but not sinfully angry where we lose control.

Ephesians 4:26a NIV
"In your anger do not sin"

If you are not completely composed and calm when your child has been disobedient or disrespectful, then you have no right to discipline them. You have disqualified yourself in that moment from being the disciplinarian that you should be in that given situation. If you are not faithful in consistent discipline there will be consequences. You will not be obeying God and they will not learn respect and obedience. They will most likely not learn to respect you, other authorities and ultimately God. Our job is to nurture them into becoming wonderful adults that contribute to society, carry their own loads and ultimately love God wholeheartedly themselves. Appropriate Godly discipline is not something the world advises, so be careful not to adopt these philosophies into your parenting convictions.

Reflection:

Q: Have you ever disciplined your children in anger and sinned? If so, have you repented?

Below are some Biblical principles concerning disciplining our children:

Proverbs 13:24 NKJV
He who spares his rod hates his son, But he who loves him disciplines him promptly.

Proverbs 13:1 NLT
A wise child accepts a parent's discipline; a mocker refuses to listen to correction.

Proverbs 19:18 NIV
Discipline your children, for in that there is hope; do not be a willing party to their death.

Proverbs 22:15 NIV
Folly is bound up in the heart of a child, but the rod of discipline will drive it far away.

Proverbs 23:13-14 NIV
Do not withhold discipline from a child; if you punish them with the rod, they will not die. [14] Punish them with the rod and save them from death.

Proverbs 29:17 NIV
Discipline your children, and they will give you peace; they will bring you the delights you desire.

Having a conviction on something means that you are practicing it. It is true that "the apple doesn't fall far from the tree", so in many ways we adopt the parenting we received. It is imperative for parents to work together and be unified in their approach to specifics concerning discipline and parenting overall.

Sometimes parents become neglectful in disciplining their children based on their own childhood abuse and trauma. The fact that anyone is abused is heartbreaking and sadly these statistics are staggering. It is understandable to be hesitant if you grew up in a dysfunctional violent family. However, simply throwing your hands in the air and failing to take action is not the Godly approach either. We must deal with our own triggers and baggage in order to heal and be Godly parents. (See the chapter on mind renewal in Part 3 of this workbook series for further specifics on how to deal with pain). As disciples, God counsels us to discipline our children. God would never ask of us what He does not enable in us.

Reflection:

Q: Do you have unresolved fears or other issues towards discipline? If so, what are they?

Q: Will you take the necessary steps to start renewing your mind in order to heal?

Q: Do you have a Godly conviction on disciplining your children and are you consistent in doing so?

Q: Who's counsel are you yielding based on the way you train and discipline your children today?

ARE YOU PUSHING DRUGS ONTO YOUR CHILD?

Talk to any college student and ask them if they or their friends take adderall? Another guilty party to the psychotropic drug pandemic are the parents who live vicariously through their children. I had a dear Sister who works in the medical field tell me that parents come into the clinic demanding that their children be prescribed adderall because their grades are not what they could be. Can you imagine this? Parents are counseling their precious children to take addictive prescription drugs! We live in a fallen world and must be very vigilant in order to avoid the "short cut" schemes readily available.

Some new parents are embracing the label of ADHD for their energetic young children, even at 2 years old, and agreeing to put them on ritalin (this drug is one chemical short of cocaine). Their claims are that they are "hard to handle", "too active" and "do not focus and obey". Fellow Disciples of Jesus, this is a problem!

ARE THEY LEARNING ABOUT SEX ISSUES FROM YOU OR FROM THE WORLD?

Another huge subject of controversy in our society is sex. The practicals of why God created sex and what boundaries He set. The truth about abortion. The topics of homosexuality and all the transgender issues.

Pornography, a huge problem and sadly readily accessible to all worldwide. These along with women's rights, wholesome speech, marijuana use and many more are all issues our children will encounter. As disciple parents we are responsible to teach and train our children, directing them to God's counsel. Teachers, professors, social media, philosophers, therapists and even some who claim to be "pastors" can have all kinds of unbiblical convictions that they readily promote.

Colossians 2:8 NIV
See to it that no one takes you captive through hollow and deceptive philosophy, which depends on human tradition and the elemental spiritual forces of this world rather than on Christ.

God recognizes us in the womb as he knits us together, one cell at a time. I am shocked at "Christians" that support abortion.

Psalm 139:13-16 NIV
For you created my inmost being; you knit me together in my mother's womb. [14] I praise you because I am fearfully and wonderfully made; your works are wonderful, I know that full well. [15] My frame was not hidden from you when I was made in the secret place, when I was woven together in the depths of the earth. [16] Your eyes saw my unformed body; all the days ordained for me were written in your book before one of them came to be.

Godly teachings   **VERSUS**   **Ungodly teachings**

One of the main stumbling blocks for my daughter in becoming a true disciple was that she had many bisexual and homosexual friends at school and felt like if she became a disciple she was somehow discriminating against them. The teachings our children are receiving included "love is love" and "don't be a hater". This propaganda had her doubting God's Word. Our children are falsely indoctrinated at school, via television and on social media. This is the counseling they are being bombarded with. They desire to fit in with their peers and so taking a stand for what is right is understandably very daunting to them. We must teach them the truth unapologetically. Disciples do not hate anyone, ever. However, we do not agree with sinful choices. Any sex, except between a man and a woman married to each other, is sinful. Period. The Bible is written at a 6th grade level, we complicate it when our vision gets blurred by the lies of the world.

1 Corinthians 6:9-10 TLB
Don't you know that those doing such things have no share in the Kingdom of God?
Don't fool yourselves. Those who live immoral lives, who are idol worshipers, adulterers
or homosexuals-will have no share in his Kingdom. Neither will thieves or greedy people,
drunkards, slanderers, or robbers.

If your child starts dressing contrary to their gender, you need to wisely correct them. This does not mean that our girls have to wear lace and frills but counseling them gently into finding their own style within the gender God has gifted them, is our responsibility. We cannot buy into the lie that whatever anybody chooses to do or be is great because that's how they were born or identify! If you refer to a male as a she or an it you are lying since a male is not a female - this is Biblical and common sense. Neither is a female a male. Use your common sense! Let's see how God feels about liars.

Proverbs 12:22 NIV
The LORD detests lying lips, but he delights in people who are trustworthy.

My daughter got baptized as a true disciple at age 16 and chose to adopt God's truth above popular opinion. She is one of the best examples I know of love and encouragement. She still has friends who live alternative lifestyles, they know where she stands about their choices being wrong. They also know that she loves them and always keeps the door to God's way open. Let's not forget that love, not judgment, never fails (1 Cor 13:8). We cannot buy into the world's approach on what is right and how to be healthy in order to function optimally.

Some parents are just overwhelmed at how to approach these and other topics and subsequently allow distraction and life to defer their attention elsewhere. I can relate to being overwhelmed as a parent. I am thankful for the direction in God's Word as well as all the advice shared with us. Parenting perhaps is much like serving in the peace corps, "the hardest job you'll ever love"! Thankfully there are also other wonderful resources out there such as the book series described below.

The "God's Design for Sex" series by Stan and Brenna Jones is a Christian perspective guide aimed at helping parents educate their children about the topic of sex in an age-appropriate manner. The series includes several volumes tailored to different age groups, beginning with the basics of human anatomy and reproduction, and progressively addressing topics such as relationships, emotional development, and God's purpose for sex within the context of marriage. Included are the topics of homosexuality as well as gender orientation. The books emphasize a positive, biblically-based understanding of sexuality, encouraging open communication between parents and children. They aim to equip children with knowledge, values, and a framework that aligns with Christian beliefs regarding love, respect, and the sacredness of human intimacy. Through engaging illustrations and accessible language, the series fosters discussion about God's design for sex, helping children to develop a healthy and holy view of their bodies and relationships. Each volume is designed to be used by parents to navigate conversations in a way that is respectful to the child's maturity and understanding.

Some other great books are: "Before I was Born" by Carolyn Nystrom, "Good Pictures Bad Pictures" by Kristen A Jenson, "Gospel-Centered Family by Paul David Tripp, "Love the Little Children: A Study of Abortion" by Kristine McGuire and "Shepherding a Child's Heart" by Ted Tripp.

Reflection:

Q: Have you conformed to the pattern of the world in your own convictions on these very controversial issues?

Q: Do your children know where you stand and why?

Q: Are you compromising in any way in your parental responsibilities to teach and discipline your children? If so, how?

As a parent, I have sinned against my children when I have failed to give them adequate attention, instruction and appropriate discipline. For this I have apologized to them humbly. I have also always prayed for them and asked God and those around me for wisdom to do my best to raise them His way. To this day I am fully engaged in loving them with the love I continue to receive from God, regardless of their choices as adults. As our children grow up they develop their own convictions one way or another. We cannot push our faith onto our adult children, neither should we be condemning them. Once you have kindly and gently shared your concerns with your adult children continue to give them your heart and stay fully invested in them. Never forget that "love never fails" (1 Cor 13:8a).

As Godly parents we can only control ourselves at the end of the day. Let's do so by gaining and maintaining Godly standards based on the truth in the Word alone. Let us not be deceived into complying with anything that contradicts His counsel.

Reflection:

Q: Do you practice humility towards your children? If so, how? When was the last time you apologized to your child? If so, how?

In Summary:

Our children are a reward and a responsibility from God. We must pay careful attention to training them in the way of the Lord and make sure we do not cower otherwise, regardless of how controversial the issues may be. Hold unswervingly to the promises of God, pray fervently, seek Godly counsel and simply do the best you can. God will do the rest. Remember that we serve a good God, a very good God!

Enjoy the journey of being a Godly parent

Conclusion

Having walked with me through Part 1 my heartfelt prayer for you, dear Reader, is that you will discover - fresh each day - that Jesus is your most treasured relationship. In that discovery, may God ignite in you a passion, or rekindle the zeal you once had, to always: "Grow, Baby grow!"

When I made Jesus my Lord and Savior, I embraced the clear vision of the two greatest commandments. To love God with my whole being and to love others as I love myself. Over the next couple of decades my perspective gradually blurred - distractions, demands and a variety of suffering clouded my focus. I slowly became entangled in the "busy-ness" of life and the motions of "spiritual activity," mistaking movement for maturity. In God's mercy, He used pain to get my attention - slowing me down to teach me the value of intentionally maturing versus simply getting older.

In this 3 Part Workbook Series I share in detail what helps me to continue to grow up spiritually. Part 1 emphasised loving Jesus as our Lord, Savior and best Friend. We flourish when we prioritize nourishing the Holy Spirit within us. In Part 2 we will examine loving ourselves as God loves us and how to steward our physical bodies accordingly. Part 3 discusses loving our souls - how to regulate incoming information, manage our emotions and renew past traumas.

I invite you to return to the principles in Part 1 as often as you need to and to approach Parts 2 and 3 with equal prayerfulness, fervor and commitment.

Let's love our Lord by constantly maturing spiritually - growing in **Self Control over SPIRIT, BODY AND SOUL**.

To our almighty God be all the glory!

> **"Your choices today will determine your tomorrow."**
> **- Unknown**

I NEED

~~to~~ ~~make more~~ money

~~to~~ ~~have~~ more business

~~to~~ ~~get~~ ~~more~~ followers

~~to~~ ~~be happier~~

~~to~~ ~~get things~~ done

~~to~~ ~~be the BEST~~

~~to~~ ~~BE PERFECT~~

Jesus.

www.ingramcontent.com/pod-product-compliance
Lightning Source LLC
Chambersburg PA
CBHW080452030726
47592CB00011B/3077